Ken S

You Again

LAST POEMS

& OTHER WORDS

BLOODAXE BOOKS

ISBN: 1 85224 670 7

First published 2004 by
Bloodaxe Books Ltd,
Highgreen,
Tarset,
Northumberland NE48 1RP.

www.bloodaxebooks.com
For further information about Bloodaxe titles
please visit our website or write to
the above address for a catalogue.

Bloodaxe Books Ltd acknowledges
the financial assistance of
Arts Council England, North East.

Cover printing by J. Thomson Colour Printers Ltd, Glasgow.

Printed in Great Britain by
Cromwell Press Ltd, Trowbridge, Wiltshire.

YOU AGAIN

KEN SMITH (1938–2003)
PHOTO: PETE STIFF

KEN SMITH IN NEWCASTLE, 1985
PHOTO: MOIRA CONWAY

CONTENTS

ACKNOWLEDGEMENTS

Acknowledgements are due to the editors of the following publications in which some of the *Last Poems* first appeared: *Ambit, Notre Dame Review* ('The Ring'), *Poetry London, Poetry Review* and *The Rialto*. 'Ancient Lights' was commissioned as part of *Performing Buildings: Six Poets, Six Buildings*, Ken Smith's building being the offices of the Royal Society of Architecture in London.

An earlier version of Roger Garfitt's 'Ken Smith: *The Poet Reclining*' was published in *Dictionary of Literary Biography: Poets of Great Britain and Ireland Since 1960*, vol. 40 (Detroit & Michigan: Gale Research Inc, 1985). Jon Glover's 'Ken Smith: *Terra* to *Shed*' draws on an obituary published in *The Guardian* on 3 July 2003. Colin Raw's interview with Ken Smith appeared in *The Catalogue* (Bloodaxe Books, 1998); his essay and the letter extracts are previously unpublished.

'Ken Smith etc' was written for Worcester County Poetry Association (Massachusetts) for a broadsheet produced for a reading on 4 December 1972. 'Ken Smith comments' is reprinted from *Contemporary Poets*, 5th edition, ed. Tracy Chevalier (Chicago & London: St James Press, 1991). 'Invisible Thread [#2]' was an editorial piece in *South West Review* (May 1978), not to be confused with the prose sequence of the same title in *A Book of Chinese Whispers*. 'Dark Jokes' (on *Terra*), 'Getting a Result' (*Wormwood*), '*The heart, the border*', 'Masks and Mirrors' (*Tender to the Queen of Spain*) and 'Swag-bag of a word-thief (*Wild Root*) were commissioned by the Poetry Book Society and first published in the *PBS Bulletin*. 'Why I write' appeared in *the text* (issue 6, 1997). The other prose pieces are probably first published here.

The previously published poems interwoven with the prose pieces in the *Other Words* section are reprinted from Ken Smith's *The Poet Reclining: Selected Poems 1962-1980* (Bloodaxe Books, 1982) and *Shed: Poems 1980-2001* (Bloodaxe Books, 2002).

The poems for Ken by Tom Pickard, Sean O'Brien, Michael Anania and Tony Connor were first published in *Foolscap*.

Special thanks are due to Judi Benson and Colin Raw, without whose help this book would not have had half as many poems and other words, and to Ken and Judi's family for many of the photos.

LAST POEMS

Ken launching Shed *in his shed, August 2002* (photo: tim cumming).

Late night call

Discontinued voice from a disconnected number
in distant rainy Seattle, you're sitting on a balcony,
smoking in another no-smoking house, out there
in the time zones. We're out of sync.

Just a faint hum on the horizon of listening,
babble of electronics and the slow hiss of static.

Once upon a time you walked into the room of my life
and changed all the seating arrangements.

You with your blue eyes. My marjoram,
my lumpy gravy. Staring at the rain.

Ancient Lights

Through the shadows and the street cries scribbler Boswell,
as ever in need of a drink and an eye out for the ladies,
limping along beside him old Dictionary Johnson,
as ever in need of a bath. Ghosts in the traffic,
shadows in dim lamplight turning off the Strand,
headed for the lit door of No. 8, there in the Great Room
to attend a lecture on light, and after to the tavern.

Sirs, we are made of light, all of light. And I?
I am the doorkeeper to this house of enlightenment,
though I am long gone into the sunset now, I am but his ghost
among the other ghosts, the company of ancient lights.

Beneath all this noble talk up above of improvement,
I know the other trades thriving underneath
in the tunnels and the arches down below,
down where the river's traffic in wines from the lowlands,
coals from Newcastle, roll up the cobbles on iron wheels
among gulls' cries and women's, rats, dogs,
the odd corpse knocking at the wharfside,
and the black slave boy sneaked by at nightfall, hooded,
lost in the city's night and the fogs of the riverside,
I saw him scurried by just as that moment
Dogood Franklin handing in his coat muttered
to himself liberty, liberty, what is liberty but an engine
that must be fuelled and from which much use comes.

Years go by into centuries. I've met them all.
Reynolds, that toff, I have shaken the rain from his umbrella.
Adam Smith, I have taken his coat and he thanked me.
Marx, never a tipper, nor stood any man a drink.
Stephenson, now there was a gentleman, and the likes
of Isambard Kingdom Brunel we'll not see again,
nor your man Charlie Dickens, forever declaring
Brighten it, brighten it, a man always departing in haste.
And that wee man, the unknown inventor of a writing desk
that in case of shipwreck opens out into a literati,
he gave me the name of a very fine horse once.

So here's to all and all the others anonymous,
may they be blessed and ever of good cheer
who set out to make this world more sensible,
at any rate from where I stand here in the doorframe.

You again

These days of terror I daren't write anything,
or I don't want to, but here you are again,
Sarah, in my waking dreams out in the street
in the midday where suddenly you enter my mind again.

Whispering, your last breath a soft quick *no no*
at my ear, and *Sarah, Sarah, my name was Sarah.*
It seems there's no room in Paradise
or it doesn't exist anyway, so it's you Kenneth John.

In another war I wrote *A fool's work*
to make anything of this, a liar's to make nothing.
And you, you're in the pixels on the screen
bursting with fire. You're in the printout, somewhere.

The sound of you still in the airwaves, on file,
on the web, the net, the desktop, the database,
zipped, unzipped, encrypted, compacted,
but not ever I promise you deleted, erased.

A name in a very long list, beginning with S.
Amongst those names I will find you.
I will go looking for what days are left me, Sarah.
I promise. I promise you.

The 72 virgins question

As I understand it, those who die as martyrs for the great mad cause of the Believers go immediately to Paradise, there to gawp at the angels and the fine plumage of the birds and eat delicious foods, where for eternity they will have the tender and erotic attentions of 72 virgins. What I've not been able to discover is who originated this theory, now resident in the minds of so many testosterone-and-fundamentalism filled young Muslim men. Is it in the Koran? For them, this is the reward for flying aeroplanes into tall buildings, and slaughtering thousands at their work stations.

I have a few questions, however:

How was the figure of 72 arrived at? Why 72? Does 72 hold any particular significance, like Douglas Adams' 42, the answer to everything? Any connection with the tradition that only the camel knows the 72 names of God?

Given the recent sudden influx of martyrs into Paradise, is the supply of virgins sufficient to the purpose? Is there, in Paradise, an infinite supply of virgins?

Are any of them boy virgins? What proportion, if any?

Given the length of eternity, how long, and how, do they remain virgins?

Given the length of eternity, I would think even 72 virgins would get tedious. Are they all dropdead gorgeous? Do they grow old, or, if they stay forever young, what would there be to talk about after the event? How long before the martyrs start straying, coveting their neighbours' virgins? And think of all that bickering and scheming.

What if the martyr is a woman? Does she get the same privileges. and how does that go down with the lads back at the base?

Another question. The investigators think not all of the 19 hijackers knew they were going to die, and only six left letters behind them, so far as they know. The others just thought they were going on a jolly hijacking spree, and weren't in the full loop. So: If the martyr doesn't know he's about to die, is he eligible for the same rewards as the one who does?

And then another question. At the chemical plant that blew up on the same day in Toulouse, now thought to have been a terrorist act also, they say they found the body of a Tunisian who worked there, wearing four pairs of underpants. This is then said to have something to do with preparations for paradise, and the aforesaid virgins?

What does it have to do with it?

Where in Holy Writ does it say one pair of underpants per 18 virgins?

Bin Laden is Ken Smith

This is from the wilder shores of cyberspace, from a site called Terrorist Watch. This bit of the conspiracy theory centres on a place called New Era in Portland, Oregon that acted as a cover for a terror base whereat many of the infamous heros of Hamas, Hizbollah, al Qaeda, etc etc appeared from time to time, including bin Laden. That's what it says here, anyway. It says:

Usama bin Laden initially showed himself at New Era under the guise of a nondescript backyard mechanic type named 'Mike'. His chosen cover for the late hours in which he worked over a handmade forge, and the huge volume of propane he used while melting down his precious plutonium was that he was recycling aluminium transmissions. At the rate of over 500 gallons of propane every week, that would have made for some very valuable aluiminium.

However, it was Usama's characterization of himself as that of a tall, lanky Missouri man called Ken Smith that allowed him to appear natural... ...the only difference between bin Laden and Ken Smith is the color change of his hair, and the fact that Ken Smith had no accent.

My name has been hijacked. I expect the CIA to come knocking at my door. And what about the plutonium? Should I see a doctor? Should I turn myself in?

From semtex to anthrax

Semtex: you blow up and burst, causing collateral damage.
Smallpox: you shrink from it, you shrink away to nothing.
Pox: you don't want it, whatever it is. See Durex below.
Pax: yes indeedy brothers and sisters and mad dogs, peace, dammit.
Prolix: you just keep banging on the way I am. So I've got it.
   Look out here it comes.
Hoax: you believe every rumour and spread it.
Perspex: you're invisible. People see right through you.
Pyrex: you get very hot, and people can still see through you.
Syntax: first the pleasure, then you get to pay for it.
Durex: no more offspring.
Bisquix: this is safe. Make pancakes for breakfast.
Detox: a period of being very dry and edgy. Don't drink, don't smoke.
Tux: an eternity of tuxedos, high school proms, virgins, 72 in number.
Box: you get brain damage from this. Then you're in one. Forever.
Lax: you don't care any more, roll another one, just like the other one.
Wax: you turn into a masochist. Forty of these is enough.
Latex: you go all rubbery and inert.
Aertex: you're full of holes. Your're a string vest.
Ilex: you turn into a tree, a very fine tree.
Playtex: you turn into a girl in a girdle.
Essex: you turn into a girl in a big bra.
Middlesex: you can work this one out for yourself.
Wessex: your location is imaginary, but absolutely real.
Kotex: you start to bleed once a month.
Lurex: you shine in the dark but you have great legs.
Redsox: your spelling goes haywire. Three strikes and you're out.
   Or in.
Rollodex: you've got it, all of it, right there, but you just can't find
   it right now.
Remix (1): you say the same things in different order, like the President does.
Remix (2): you think you're the Prime Minister, and say the same
   things as
Remix (1) (above), playing an imaginary concertina with your hands,
   saying over and over *you see you see…*
Affix: you stick close to tactile surfaces.
Rolex: you get mugged.
Complex: don't go there. Just don't bother.
Reflex: see above.

Styx: there neither. Don't cross that river.

Pandora's Box: don't open it.

Halifax: don't go there. Hull, Hell, and Halifax, avoid these.

ExLax: come again?

Amex: you turn into a Mexican.

Tex: you turn into a Texan and get to be President.

Texmex: get out of there fast fat boy, stop singing those cowboy songs.

Lox: you can only eat Kosher.

Four X: you turn into an Australian, and don't give a XXXX for anything.

Max, as in Bigmax: problems with spelling again. Don't go there either.

Matrix: uh oh, lifetime hallucination, don't go there.

Tyrannosaurus rex: don't mess with him. He'll have you for breakfast.

Rex: you think you're the king, and master of all you survey.

Dux: now you think you're Mussolini. It's just the quacking of the crowd you hear.

Lex: so now you're a lawyer?

Pontifex: so now you think you're the Pope. All together now *Pax in urbe et orbi.*

Cicatrix: well you're sick anyway.

Moulinex: mixes you up completely. You're either a mess or a good mayonnaise.

Fedex: expect unexpected packages, rapidly delivered, contents unknown. Don't open.

Fax: few of these these days I find. Fog of war etc, first casualty etc etc.

Tax: you give a lot more money to the government to pay for all this.

X: unknown, too terrible to name. Marks the spot. His mark.

X-ray: people can see through you.

My ex: here's one I made earlier. What was her name?

Anthrax: was that really her name?

Vortex: you just go down and down and down.

Subtext: one way or another, I fear we're exed, four exed. Banjaxed.

The Ring

Scenes from a Civil War, Exeter, 1640s

She threw her wedding ring high in the air,
far into the night grass of the graveyard.

And I, one eye on her, one eye on its quick glint
spinning in moonlight, followed and found it.

Gold, thought I to myself, solid gold:
hot dinners, a bed, a warm winter jacket.

There we parted, the wife of those days and I.
She went her way. I went nowhere

*

I looked for a grave and found none.
Wind, rain, moss, lichen
had wiped even their names from their stones.

All faces are soon erased: neighbours,
friends, lovers, not one of all these
in the town I once knew I know now.

Kings and saints on the battered face
the cathedral presents to the west wind,
sandstone wearing away in the rain,

slowly down time, their gestures
making some fine point of doctrine
in the centuries of their long discussions.

And within there the saint's nose kissed away,
the bishop's effigy slashed,
hacked, arms, face, feet, gone.

Children who are long away
into the oncoming cannonade,
their cries that are long lost.

Townsmen I knew, scattered now, fled,
dead some, one who was my sworn enemy
whose grave I swore to piss on.

But I can't be doing with that now,
and where is it anyway?

*

Late at night as in the old times,
the last drink poured and the tabaccy low,
the clock's tick and the rain's drumming,
and I sit pondering my fortune, or lack of it.

Maybe I should not have come back here
to this town of my defeats and betrayals.
I should have passed by on the other side.
I should have kept to my wanderer's track.

Yet I am always connecting up the dots,
stitching up the tears in my coat sleeve.
In all this rattle of traffic I can easily forget
there was once something called silence.

Here it was that I as I was then,
just coming into being, knowing myself
numbered among the quick, there came
trouble and turbulence. Here I fled from.

And all fell apart. Wandering the town
and its rainy alleys, I met lads tooting pipes
that were the organ flutes of the great church,
and they jeered me, out of all command.

Years gone, I'm drawn back, into old doorways,
staring to the hill's line, the leaning
of one house on another, and the western wind
again on my cheeks, and always the rain.

Here in a lit doorway a man steps away
into his own shadow and is never seen again.
Here in an early window another lights his taper
and takes down his books of close scrutiny.

At the bar suspect conversations: money & property.
As ever. Always money to be made from grief.
I observe preachers and lawyers sow war's seeds.
Lawyers and preachers gather its whirlwind.

*

And I thinke those that crie Goddes worde
to bee lawe absolute, suche wordes
ever subject to variation and errore
in translation from tongue to tongue;

subject to sundrie interpretation thereof,
depending which way downwind they drift,
subject to weather, the mood on the high road;

subject to primers' error, faint hearing, bile,
bad eyesight, bad temper, indigestion,
the sudden sputter of the early morning candle.

Those I say who cry out Goddes goodness to all,
commanding obedience to the Boke's command
they do not sleep in a windy hedgeback
I have observed them doe the most harm.

*

That evening in the cathedral,
the notes of the organ's flutes
rippling over the high arches,
the great pillars rising into gloom
and the choir's voice fading out
into silence, the night forming
into a solid as the sun went down
beyond the coloured glass saints,
and as the dark and the music
flooded God's great barn
stacked with so many prayers
for so many centuries, then when
a single candle was lit on the altar,
I at that moment as the great world
turned into night and the fear of it,
would have believed anything.

*

All day then I stood barking wares on the market,
and at night in my fair hand transcribed
lists of ordnance, and the new regulations.
Aye and many a long crawl through the taverns,

In these fragments my life is, somewhere.
I recall one who died here on the quays,
crushed under a boat's keel, lightning
took another, others went under wheels.

Had I siblings, predecessors, antecedents,
a line all the way to Adam and the apple?
Will there be offspring of my offspring,
some of my own blood to wander the future?

Here on this bench, long ago in summer,
as I sank a slow cider, my youngest daughter
sweet Kate, was discovering the writing of her hand
its confident slopes and downsweeps, its cursives.

Adapted from my hand as mine was from Milly
my mother's as hers from her father's
copperplate entries in the history of calligraphy,
that elegant style they used then.

*

Someone whistling on the corner.
Voices outside the window,
if there is a window, when in these times
someone is always listening.

For what?

For private thoughts in late night cups
mutterings against God and the godly
damn Parliament and God damn the King.
For that fined or sent to the jailhouse.

For what?

All talk then was munitions and the price of meat,
Neighbour cast a curious eye on neighbour.
No joy was to be had in those times to come
only worse in the savage toing and froing

Sometime they locked the cathedral,
God they said, needs no such room but the heart
nor the great bells they melted into bullets.
They had other uses for such vast spaces.

Then it was divided between two parties,
and a wall set over the middle, a new door cut.
Then it was storehouse, stables, stalls,
a jakes for the beastly exonerating of natures.

That last winter they pulled down the thatch
against fire, and for fire to warm themselves
took everything else: doors, lintels, floors,
a fine chair I had from my grandfather.

*

No question ever answered,
no thought ever finished.

I think we just fade out
across whatever borderland we come to.

A while we go on, buying milk,
bread, wine, filling the shaker with salt.

Good morning a fine morning,
crossing the bridge into the city.

We do the same things in the same order,
in summer's heat imagining winter's cold.

And vice versa. So this is the after life
of my life. Already this is it.

*

23

Our world over, we withdraw into the wind,
into the throaty susurration of pigeons,
chitter of birdsong, chatter of the high grass.

We are a flicker of light in the shadows,
breath of a sudden breeze on a still afternoon,
something glimpsed at the eye's corner

that when looked at is merely imaginary,
a fiction, an invention in the air, what the eye
wants to see, as it does, days out on the ocean.

Always on the cusp of some thought
that evaporates, the verbs falling from the nouns,
the sentence running out of sense.

To both sides I went for an ill paid soldier,
cut, shot at, wounded, slept in snowy ditches
without a warm coat, at the end without shoes.

At the last caught on the wrong side sent away.
Land and sea then were all my adventures.
Here only the exile of he who returns.

Fragments. My life's bits.
Scraps of memory. Disconnections.
I say this and I say no more.

*

She threw her wedding ring high in the air,
far into the night grass of the graveyard.

And I, one eye on her, one eye on its quick glint
spinning in moonlight, followed and found it.

Gold, thought I to myself, solid gold:
hot dinners, a bed, a warm winter jacket.

Thus we parted, the wife of those days and I.
She went her way. I went nowhere

Almost

IM Izet Sarajlic

Izet, Izet, I regret
I have not written my words
to your words, to your courage,
to your love, to your pain,
to your child's mysterious smile
in your old man's face
under its wild white hair.

To your wounds.

And Sarajevo's,

Not yet.

*

Everything, almost

A slow life in the fast lane
what with everyone in a hurry,
boring, boring my grandchildren say
of almost everything.

Everything is moving away, waving,
waving, flags, stars, flowers in the wind,
handkerchiefs from the boat's rail,
the signal fading as the land falls off,
a far window glinting in the sunlight
a single gull riding the air's weight.

Goodbye, goodbye. Everything
in its sudden intensity, the blue cup,
the black bench, the empty bottle,
the white stairs going up.

*

Begins like this

This is the almost poem, the not yet poem,
maybe the never to be poem. Perhaps.

It begins over beer with the Polish girl,
already bedded with one of three at the table.

To me she says *Ken, I could almost be in love with you.*
Here we go. Almost? Only almost? So then:

we almost could go to bed, almost make love,
by the morning you could be almost pregnant.

By the morning you would almost have forgotten me
By the same token I'd have forgotten you, almost.

Or. We could almost have a love affair,
you could almost have our children, and I,

I could almost go to Warsaw, a flat almost in Stari Grad.
One day I might almost forget the wife I had.

The life I live already, the one I'm not waiting
any more to start beginning one day but now.

Her Indoors we call her in my lingua franca,
Miss Peaches I call her still, almost this moment

of the same evening gathering tomatoes, planted
months ago in our garden at the house back,

quieter just now without my heavy footsteps.
She'd never forgive me nor forget me. Almost,

I would most certainly have a fight with your husband.
He might almost kill me, I almost him.

And you, you'd almost come to see me, one Sunday,
in the hospital or in the jail or in the cemetery.

Almost you might bring flowers. You might
almost remember me. Otherwise I'd almost kill you

for your endless infidelities. Almost.
For your carelessness with what love is.

*

26

Nema problema

Doesn't work. Nothing works.
Almost everything lost in translation.
The wrong word in the wrong sentence,
wrong coin in the wrong pocket,
by the omission of a letter,
the variation of a constant, said Vishnu.

And you're stuck here forever perhaps
among the unknown alphabets
between the mountains and the sea
waiting for the ship that never sails,
the office never open, the phone not picked up,
the recorded voice far away offering options
in umpteen languages, none of them your own.

And it's your own fault, dummy, waving your arms about.
What time is the bus? What time is the bus?

You may be this way again o mi amigo,
so behave yourself, you with a stick
you like to think is a gun.

OK amigo, you got me scared now.

Nema problema.
No problem.
Niet problem.
Kein Problem.
Es neme probleme.
Pas de problème.
No hay problema.
Mish mushkila.

They say. Tell that to the marines blacking up
for yet another war, tell that to the gunmen in the hills.

Kindly inform the poor kneeling at the roadside,
palms up, eyes fixed on the almost endless empty distance forever.

*

27

Nightbird

At midnight the full moon over Lake Orhid,
its full light scattered over sheer still water,
tiny waves sifting the pebbles of the shoreline
with a *shush now* sound, hard to find a word for.

As is the sudden soft throaty cry of a nightbird,
just overhead, its wings soughing the balmy air
in a splash of feathers, like a passing prayer:
Let there be peace in this land. Peace, now.

*

Listening

to the last ashes of any sound at all,
a vague music fading in the courtyards,
the announcement of twilight in the mouths of birds,
in the bus stations the destinations to distant cities,
Mostar, Vukovar, Sarajevo, Banja Luka,
in all their names in all their tongues,
with all their bloody histories, and all this
only the immediate neighbourhood,
and whatever lies further out beyond the last lights
along the Albanian shore we've not yet figured out.

All this to the last breath you take anywhere. Almost,

Oh and there was something else:
what would anyone want beyond food enough,
warmth, some promise, some love
on this mean miserable planet, anything at all
that is your gift to your children and to theirs,
some shelter from almost all of the above.

*

Split interlude at deadmouse.com

Ok the keyboard is differently configured.
Ok there's no sign for infinity, but you get there,
you write over and over *I love you love you,*
I'm not in jail, I'm alive, I'm not sick.

Hit Send. For what we are about to send and receive
may the Lord make us truly thankful. Doesn't work.
Must enter identity the man says. *Make password.*
Any word will do. Almost any word almost.

But the mouse is dead. *Dead mouse* he says,
fiddling at the back, *very old late ex mouse.*
And no spare. *Nema problema.* So my message
I love you won't arrive in your inbox. Ever.

*

Night coming

Travel torn, sitting on a balcony
watching the heavy Dalmatian rain
lash the streets, boats tossing on the swell,
thunder rolling in, lightning's swift stitchery
in the steep bowls of the hills
when all the lights go out.
                              Suddenly
I am content, not almost but utterly,
soon to fall asleep alone in white sheets
rocking in the windy cradle of the harbour,
the sleep of an angel that is once in ten thousand years
to wake as if born again almost, still dreaming.

How tentative our lives, how short a time in the sunlight,
and most of it imaginary elsewheres, Dubrovnik for instance.

*

Things

The way they have their own particularities,
left alone long enough, their solitude, silence,
fullness and emptiness, their togetherness and
their autonomies, their connection to everything else.

The stone.

The rusty horse shoe and one nail.

The abandoned suitcase.

The lost doll on the roadside.

The rake the saw the hammer, tools that were his tools.

The empty Coca Cola can in a half-built house in Sobra,
the rope coiled on the quayside, a one spit, one shoe,
one shot, one last cigarette port call if ever I saw one.

The spent police bullet found in the gravel at Castle Stanjel.

The fallen chestnut.

The fallen leaf from a gingko tree
by the old synagogue in Sarajevo.

The bone.

Everything.

*

Seafarer

landward mountains and mountains, upended strata
tipped all the way up the coastline of what was
an almost country, almost Yugoslavia. Islands
that are mountains in the sea, the same in the same
dark blue waters the ancient wanderer spread sail on,
ten years lost, the waves cresting the same, bright
sunlight's swift jewellery forming and fast fading,
wind never willing enough, always far from home.
Not even almost there, the boat's wake always behind him.
So if not home then some haven beyond the next headland,

round the next cape almost, sunlight striding the sea
receding always into sea haize and more distance.

Home to his ancient dog and the wife's endless weaving,
not to mention the slaughterhouse he soon made of it.
Tales told round fires, late night yarns over alcohol,
trying some sense to this endless confusion of water.
Waves, tentative, foam crests soon falling, seamen
staring the sea down for some place looks like home
and the stars above in the right configurations,
wind whipped and sea blind, he sees in the sea's skin
forever on the move sight of the sun through pines
in the bright sea's reflections as it once was on land,
the motion the same as the same wind's back home,
almost. The endless immensity of longing for home.

Almost. Rocks, trees, beasts, faces of the familiar,
rearing from stone, out of water, wood, smoke, rock, clouds
out of yesterday's brisk trade in the town, flash ahead of him
gone. And below where light strikes, snakes, almost,
creatures writhing away into seaspray and light shine.
Words on the sea. Light's brief brilliant reflections,
languages never learned, cuneiform, glagolitic, Hebrew,
Arabic, glyphs, runes, living almost into letters, tongues,
alphabets, lost in the quick calligraphy of wind and water.
The almost everything almost always is, or boils down to:
it was or it will be, could be, may be, might be, perhaps,
though doubtful. Uncertain. World on the brink of itself.

Always almost always making it, becoming itself,
being or not being, uncertain of itself. Potential, say.
Out on the sea for instance where our seafarer
almost always is. Off the bitter coast. Off Hvar
and Korcula, birthplace it says here im Deutsch
of Antenor of Troy, and of Marco the Polo, wanderer
by land to the earth's ends and limits. Or by Ogygia,
Mijet now, a long lumpy island wherein seven
of ten lost years went by: cloudy light, forest,
a single road looping the gaps. *Ah Ithaca, where
are my olives, my olive trees?* Ogygia: upright rocks,
stoney warriors armed to the teeth, no landing there.

All this, blind, long after. Homer saw.

*

On the other hand

Given a compass, Racal Decca,
geostat positioning and a decent map
there'd have been none of these adventures
and no tales to tell the grandchildren.

He'd have been tucked up night after night
with Penelope dreaming one eyed giants,
men turned to pigs. On the wind off the sea
the singing women calling him in to his ruin.

And for her none of these tapestries,
done and every night undone again.
An ordinary life, long forgotten now.
Wine in the evening. His olives.

Almost

*

Old man's advice

War: the worst dialogue there is,
all the nouns scattered body parts,
all the verbs fire. No sentence
ever gets finished. Just the abrupt
chatter of bullets, punctuation of artillery,
cluster bombs translated into collateral damage.

The wailing long after.
There's no future tense.
And never enough adjectives. A language
only of lamentation.

But they're talking it up again.
It's show time folks. Take my advice:

you go on whittling that same piece of wood
you end up out of stick, a bunch of shavings
at your feet and a blunt knife in your hand.

*

For Jan Morris

Long ago before the war we haven't had yet
there was I in Trieste. Someone had written
on a wall just off Unita in Cats' Alley
No stars for me this night.

All laughter with its edge of sorrow.
All regret with some punchline of its own.

Too many tears falling,
like the cold light from the stars.
Here. Everywhere.

*

A night of many dreams

none of which I now remember. Trumpets
perhaps, blown in some deep cave in the karst
slow water has carved into figures and faces,
the white columns of some ancient cathedral.

Almost.

Or maybe the white trotting horses of Lipica,
glimpsed in an autumn country runny with fruit,
orchards heavy with apples, pomegranate, grapes,
sticky on the fingers, the wind's songs.

Almost.

By day's end a host of faces flash by,
coming on fast as if out of rock and wood,
out of water and iron and fire, their voices
in so many languages keeping me from sleep.

Almost.

*

Almost not a sonnet

You can be the king of England and be happy, almost.
You can win the state lottery and almost be a millionaire.
You can be almost famous. You can almost die, over and over.
You can almost live. You can almost go to war with the neighbours,
or almost live in peace with them. Some days almost
you can walk on water, you can fly, you can dance the kolo again.
You can almost be in love with that girl you glimpsed in Zagreb.
A white dress, yellow braids, high heel shoes, almost evening,
the light rain almost over. Or was that Ljubljana? Almost
you could go and go forever over the landscape, always
a new town with its new adventures, its women almost
holding on to you, almost every night a different bed.
Unlimited possibilities are not given to man, saith the I Ching.
If they were his life would dissolve in the boundless.

*

I rest my case

Lizard.
Scorpion.
Pine cone.
Water falling. Wind.

I was making my way between mountains and islands,
all on my ownio, o solo mio, almost at last a bona fide grown up,
just getting there, wherever there was. Tomorrow
I could go to Hvar and wander in its woods. Or tomorrow
I could bugger off to Rijeka and get drunk. Almost.
As ever I do neither. Watch the sun come up, go down.
Sleep. Split for Split and a late night beer with Ante,
who builds ships in the yards but would rather sail them,
elsewhere, anywhere, the girl in the tourist office
who envies those she sells the tickets to: another life,
another world than this, any place almost. Some place
she'll be someone else completely. America for instance.

Wind. Water falling.
Pine cone.
Scorpion
Lizard.

I rest my case.

Poverty's prayer

Poverty's shoes, if any.
Poverty's house, falling down.
Poverty's hard bed. Poverty's sticks,

Poverty's thin cat,
poverty's dog and its fleas,
its leg in a dirty grey bandage.

Poverty's bread. Poverty's dust
Poverty's mice and cucarachas.
Poverty's rice, poverty's beans.

Por favor
bring me the head of an American president
on the green platter of a dollar bill.

[*Havana, 2003*]

The white chair

The man whose seat this is,
heavy iron, white paint, that he dragged out
one day into a corner of the rattling leaves
in the seawind, he is not here today.

He went off some place, some business,
and just now he is standing perhaps
amongst other leaves drummed on the same wind
Coming in fast off a different sea.

But he has no seat to sit in, and here
it's as if his chair was waiting for me,
among the dropped brown leaves scurrying
like small animals, like birds into flight.

So therefore I will sit here thinking of him,
someone very like me perhaps, a solitary
who likes company, wherever he is and in what language
he listens to the wind, and what it says to him.

I will disturb nothing. Back again,
he will not know I have been here,
stepping down into the evening to sit
in his chosen spot, lighting his cigar.

[*Havana, 2003*]

KEN SMITH
(1938-2003)

Ken Smith at Lumb Bank, Yorkshire, c. 1987 (PHOTO: JOE HANDLEY).

TOP LEFT: *Ken sitting left with father John and evacuee Peter, c. 1942.*
TOP RIGHT: *Ken with his father John, c. 1943/44.*
BOTTOM LEFT: *Studio photograph of Ken, 8 April 1942.*
BOTTOM RIGHT: *Ken with mother Milly and sister Julie, c. 1948/49.*

ROGER GARFITT
Ken Smith: *The Poet Reclining*
(LIFE & WORK, 1: 1938-1986)

Kenneth John Smith was born on 4 December 1938 in Rudston, a village in the North Riding of Yorkshire, the son of a farm labourer, John Patrick Smith (1904-71) and Millicent (Milly) Emma (*née* Sitch) Smith (1911-90). Harsh conditions and an unyielding temper ensured that his father never kept a job for long. The first of the wanderer figures that haunt Smith's poetry were his own family, moving on at the end of harvest:

> a darker blur on the stubble,
> a fragment in time gone, we left
> not a mark, not: a footprint.

The isolation of this life meant that he grew up 'talking to myself and inventing mates', which is where 'the habit of inventing people and dialogue, stories and fictions' began.

Solitude intensified when he moved to the city at the age of 13. The horizon shrank, the world became small and hostile. His conversation with himself became silent and turned to writing. His father had saved enough to buy a grocer's shop in Hull, an independence with which he rapidly became embittered. He prospered and bought a second shop, which Smith ran when he left school. But there were continual violent arguments, in which Smith had to defend his mother. It was a situation Smith was locked into until, at the age of 19, conscription released him.

In the Air Force he became a typist, and assuaged his boredom by reading widely and completing his university entrance qualifications. He was demobilised in the spring of 1960, returning to Hull, where he married Ann Minnis, a secretary, on 1 August. In the autumn they moved to Leeds where he read English at the university.

Leeds had become an important literary centre. The school of English included Wilson Knight, Douglas Jefferson and Geoffrey Hill, who was then teaching contemporary poetry. Jon Silkin had just completed two years as Gregory Fellow in Poetry and was now an English undergraduate himself. His successors as Gregory Fellow were William Price Turner and Peter Redgrove. Literary activity centered on the weekly magazine *Poetry and Audience*, of which Smith became assistant editor. Through *Poetry and Audience* he met Silkin and in 1963 he became a co-editor of *Stand*, an association that lasted until 1969.

TOP LEFT: *Ken, 1950s portrait.*

TOP RIGHT: *Ken aged 19, called up for National Service with the RAF in 1958.*

BOTTOM LEFT: *Ken Smith, Leeds graduation photograph, 1963.*

BOTTOM RIGHT: *Ken and grandfather Arthur Sitch with mother Milly holding Ken's firstborn, daughter Nicole, 1961.*

For a few months after graduating with a B.A. in 1963 he edited, reviewed, and wrote full-time. But his daughter Nicole had been born in 1961 and the pressure of supporting a family soon forced him into teaching, first at a school in Dewsbury (1963-64), then at Dewsbury and Batley Technical and Art College (1964-65). His son Danny was born in 1965 and his daughter Kate in 1966. In 1965 he moved south, to teach complementary studies at Exeter College of Art. The teaching proved complementary for him too. His own education had been literary and linear: from the art students he learned to think laterally, by image and association, and acquired a much sharper visual sense. It was a development that was to prove crucial to his poetry.

His first pamphlet, *Eleven Poems*, was published by Northern House in 1964 and his first collection, *The Pity*, by Jonathan Cape in 1967. *The Pity* was very well reviewed. P.J. Kavanagh wrote in the Guardian, 'Anyone who despairs of contemporary verse should be led by the hand to this book.' The most arresting poem is the title-poem, which incorporates the lines Mao Tse-tung wrote in prison when his pregnant wife was garroted in the next cell:

I cut my hands on the cords at the strangling-post
but no blood spilled from my veins;
instead of blood I watched and saw the pity run out of me.

Writing in Mao's voice, Smith gives a restrained and sensitive account of that moment of inner revolution when 'Compassion... takes the hawk's wing, diving.'

In one sense Smith's poetry was released as soon as he was free from study. He wrote 'The pity' and 'Family group' in the week that he graduated. In another sense the poems still felt like studies, the results of conscious writing strategies. Despite the achievement of *The Pity*, he felt the need to break his habits of mind, to break free from his cultural inheritance: 'Part of being English is that we entertain really only a few footholds on the imagination.'

In 1969 he moved to America, where he took up a post as writer in residence at Slippery Rock State College in Pennsylvania. Once outside England he fell free 'to take much bigger risks...to follow out ridiculous ideas...I could invent much more, push a particular image in ways that in English poetry would be regarded as luxurious.' He learned from the work of American poets: James Wright, Robert Bly, David Ignatow, William Stafford, and the Alaskan poems of John Haines.

He learned still more, perhaps, from oral and primitive poetry, in which there was a revival of interest in America at that time. His second collection, *Work, distances/poems* (Swallow Press, Chicago,

TOP: *Ken with family in Slippery Rock, Pennsylvania: wife Ann seated, daughter Nicole standing behind, Kate standing in front, son Danny sitting on floor.*

BOTTOM: *Ken in America, 1960s.*

1972), includes 'Ghost songs', 'Ghost dances', and an adaptation, 'From the Nahua': but particular borrowings are important only as indications of a deeper influence on his poetic language that persisted on his return to England. When he walks beside a playing field in Exeter and writes of

> accepting my birthday.
>
> How the shadows move in
> at such news and are strange
> in the light. This feather
> left for his marker my brother
>
> the crow had dropped by the goalpost
> seems a dead man's finger
> keeping his page
> in the unfinished biography,

he is re-entering, if only for the space of a metaphor, a universe that is a unity, where the poet can discern his own myth taking shape in correspondences, reflections, foreshadowings. Poetry ceases to be what it so often is in England, an art of framed observations: it becomes the spelling out of a selfhood, 'a language to speak to myself'. The practice of the poet becomes a matter

> of silence
> and waiting, how to forget,
> how sleep, to see and not notice
> the moment the mind
> takes to its channel, its
> leaping and threading and listening,
> the business of dreams, visions,
> and distant barely perceptible sounds
> – how they effect
> what is brought to the world's gate.

One sequence is literally 'the business of dreams'. 'The Eli poems' sprang, as Smith describes in a prose passage, 'the door', from insistent dreams of a landscape through which two figures moved, Eli, a lodging house keeper, and Kate, a mill girl he had got with child. The first poem, 'Eli's poem', was dreamed complete as a poem on a page in a book and typed out immediately on waking. The final poem, 'Half songs, 1790', came from a waking dream a year later, a daylight glimpse of Kate that was like 'a going and a showing at the same time'.

More often Smith works from a kind of personal archaeology. The sequence 'The clearing' came from exploring an actual clearing (set in 'Minnesota perhaps' but in fact in Massachusetts) and sifting through the settler's abandoned house. Once again a prose

TOP LEFT: *Back in England, Ken pictured outside Exeter Cathedral, early 1970s.*
TOP RIGHT: *Ken, 1975.*
BOTTOM: *Ken with Judi Benson in Didcot, 1979.*

passage, '*Concerning the clearing*', gives the genesis of the poems. Into this reconstructed history, the sense of 'poverty rising out of the ground', he weaves elements of his own mythology. The hawk of 'Hawk vision', who in a moment of liberation 'diving / somehow upward' vanished, now returns 'hungry, / weary, wrong-muscled, / grey bird of my death'. The fusion of personal myth with documentary material is Smith's way of relating his own life to the unity of lives, of reaffirming that he is 'a cry among cries'.

'Tales of Urias the shape-shifter', an intermittent sequence, began to take shape in Yorkshire beside Colden Water, a moorland stream that became a mill stream in the Industrial Revolution. One root of the poem is a local belief, recorded by Elizabeth Gaskell, that 'there were little people, there were spirits here...until the machinery came'. Another root is Smith's own sense of

> something very surly and crushed that for the sake of a metaphor...for the sake of a fiction you could say was the spirit of that water...My sense of the world is not much in common with my time...The universe is articulate, it is trying to speak, we are one of the agencies by which it speaks,
>
> > part of how the world thinks
> > so through us the blank
> > stuff of space knows itself.
>
> But we're not the only agency.

Here again Smith's poetry forms part of an older tradition. 'The kingdom' of which he writes is the kingdom of William Blake's grain of sand, of Thomas Traherne's Orient and immortal wheat. 'The other world' appears when we give proper attention to this world:

> Describing the buds of the sycamore
> coming out boxed each 4 to unfold
> is to be in the other world
> listening in this one.

Three years at Slippery Rock were followed by a year as poet in residence to the College of the Holy Cross and Clark University in Worcester, Massachusetts. *Work, distances/ poems*, which had been rejected by three English publishers, was well-received in America. Ralph J. Mills, writing in the *Chicago Sun-Times*, welcomed Smith as 'a poet of formidable range and strength'. Smith returned to England in 1973 but continued to travel extensively in America and to have his work published in America. He continued to be better-known in America until Bloodaxe's publication in 1982 of *The Poet Reclining: Selected Poems 1962-1980* re-established his reputation in Britain. *The Poet Reclining* is a testament to Smith's integrity and endurance. A major imaginative enterprise 'in the

TOP: *Ken with his mother Milly (left); Judi with her mother Julia (centre) and son Todd, with Ken's daughter Nicole (right). Friars Road, East Ham, 1983.*
BOTTOM: *Ken in his shed at Friars Road, c. 1989.*

American grain', it had to be sustained against the grain of contemporary English poetry.

There is no stylistic or thematic division between *Work, distances* and *The Poet Reclining* as there is between *Work, distances* and *The Pity*, and the above discussion of Smith's work ranges freely between them. But ten years separate the two volumes, ten years in which Smith became virtually an underground poet in Britain. He received an Arts Council Bursary in 1975 and from 1977 to 1979 he was the founder editor of *South West Review*. But his own work surfaced only in pamphlets. From 1976 to 1978 he was Yorkshire Arts Fellow at Leeds University, commuting from Exeter, where his wife Ann held a secretarial post. Immediately after the Leeds Fellowship was over, the marriage broke up.

Smith moved to London and into the experiences of his long poem *Fox Running* (1980), a brilliant recreation of a man under stress encountering the city. Rapid, compulsive rhythms create flicker pictures of the Underground and the seedier districts, in which Fox glimpses his double, the shadow he could so easily become:

> Faces
> mentioning defeat saying
> bankruptcy desertion failure redundancy
> lost bottle. Their light
> that had gone or never lit
> or they burned now on the lamp oil
> of necessity the pure oil
> of ageing euphoria.

All that separates them is the survival instinct, whatever it is in Fox that 'speaks / from the lengthening floor / of his blood his conviction / *not me not me jack*'. Smith finished up as a live-in barman in an Irish pub in Kilburn. As a poet he survived, in the words of Jeff Nuttall's *Guardian* review, by 'taking heartbreak in both hands and using it like bricks and mortar to build art...*Fox Running* is an astonishing leap in compositional scope'.

Through the University of Antioch in London Smith met the American writer Judi Benson and made a new home with her and her son Todd. From 1979 to 1981 he was writer in residence at Kingston Polytechnic, and they moved to East Ham.

The Poet Reclining was widely acclaimed, even critics like Peter Porter, who would be hostile to the element of projective verse in Smith's poetics, being forced into 'a new respect for his powers'. His subsequent collection *Terra* (1986) included the sequences *Hawkwood* and *The London Poems*. *Hawkwood* is based on the figure of Sir John Hawkwood, a 14th-century condottiere, whose career

TOP: *Ken and Judi at her 50th birthday party at Friars Road, 1997, with Ken's daughters Nicole (left) and Kate (right).*

BOTTOM LEFT: *Ken partying with son Danny (centre), London, 1999.*

BOTTOM RIGHT: *Ken, Judi and Todd, 2001.*

enabled Smith 'to write about war and aggression and masculinity ...under this metaphor of the wanderer'. The poems are like 'late night work Hawkwood might have done...a closed book I'm opening'. *The London Poems* are all short, 12-line poems, 'sonnets without the concluding couplet', his interest being partly formal, to see how much he could pack into three four-line stanzas.

Terra was followed by *A Book of Chinese Whispers* (1987), a collection of prose pieces. Smith's prose is closely akin to his poetry. Some ideas simply develop into prose: 'the stories are really very convoluted metaphors'. Because there was a limited market for experimental fiction, the prose pieces had only appeared in five pamphlets. *A Book of Chinese Whispers* collected these together with more recent prose, adding another dimension to the work of a poet who sees his development as a long 'learning to let be...to let a set of images or patterns or obsessions form itself into shape'.

[1985/2004]

JON GLOVER

Ken Smith: *Terra* to *Shed*

(LIFE & WORK, 2: 1986-2003)

Ken Smith's reputation was established and his readership widened by *The Poet Reclining* in 1982. To some extent his achievement paralleled the expansion and influence of Bloodaxe. His journeys were both inwards and outwards. His poems were intimately related to self-discovery as he placed himself in stranger and more demanding situations.

Terra (1986), *A Book of Chinese Whispers* and *Wormwood* (both 1987) were all published while Ken was writer-in-residence at Wormwood Scrubs prison between 1985 and 1987. These were followed in 1989 by a major prose account of prison life, *Inside Time* (with Dave Wait). He continued to travel and gather his intensely felt observations into prose and poetry, including *Berlin* (1990), on the fall of the Berlin Wall, and the poems of *The heart, the border* (1990), as well as several poem sequences for BBC radio. He travelled widely in the US, Europe and Latin America, visiting Hungary, Slovakia, Ukraine and Romania for his BBC projects, which merged poetry and speech with music and sounds recorded on location.

Later books included the collections *Tender to the Queen of Spain* (1993) and *Wild Root* (1998), as well as *Shed: Poems 1980-2001* (2002), which received wide praise from poets and reviewers in poetry magazines but not a single review in a national newspaper. Having the most significant book of his life ignored by the national press hurt him deeply, and disappointed all those admirers of his work who regarded *Shed* as one of the most important books of poetry from the second half of the 20th century. Four collections reprinted in *Shed* were Poetry Book Society Recommendations and *Wild Root* was the PBS Choice, while *Terra* was shortlisted for the Whitbread Poetry Award and *Wild Root* for the T.S. Eliot Prize. He received America's highly prestigious Lannan Award in 1997, and a Cholmondeley Award in 1998.

He continued to speak for victims of oppression, and the collaboration required for radio work was a vital counterbalance to his intense individuality. He edited, with Judi Benson, *Klaonica: poems for Bosnia* (1993), and with Matthew Sweeney, *Beyond Bedlam* (1997), a book of poems by mentally ill people. A book (with CD) of his BBC-commissioned poems from Hungary, *Wire through the Heart*, was published – in English – by Ister in Budapest in 2001.

Unlike some poets whose work is sparse, Ken Smith simply lived to write, and he was at the height of his powers when he brought Legionnaire's Disease back to London after a visit to Cuba. After four months in intensive care, he caught an infection while recovering in hospital, and died on 27 June 2003.

Like many poets of his generation, Ken Smith formed a creative symbiotic relationship with America – its landscape, history and language. While he lived for many years in London's East End, he could, perhaps, talk about the city experience only after the freedom and distances of the US and its people. His poetry offers a special insight into the world in which we now live. Highly personal yet accessible and involving, it provides a record of journeys that seem at first to be strange, distressing and unique. But many readers will continue to join him as though finding vital common ground for the first time.

Ken Smith was a great poet. He was a writer of personal experience who often reflected a sense of loss as he talked through the urban landscape. But he was also a fine poet of the visual and the present. His poems had to be heard, seen and felt, and they live on now as the visual, tactile and audible worlds of a wonderfully rich imagination. His last retrospective collection, *Shed*, published in 2002, confirmed the immense power of his poetry.

[2003]

SELECTED BIBLIOGRAPHY

Eleven Poems (Leeds: Northern House, 1964).

The Pity (London: Jonathan Cape, 1967).

Work, distances/poems (Chicago: Swallow Press, 1972).

Frontwards in a Backwards Movie (Todmorden: Arc, 1975).

Tristan Crazy (Newcastle upon Tyne: Bloodaxe Books, 1978).

Fox Running (London: Rolling Moss Press, 1980; Newcastle upon Tyne: Bloodaxe Books, 1981).

Abel Baker Charlie Delta Epic Sonnets (Newcastle upon Tyne: Bloodaxe Books, 1981).

Burned Books (Newcastle upon Tyne: Bloodaxe Books, 1981).

The Poet Reclining: Selected Poems 1962-1980 (Newcastle upon Tyne: Bloodaxe Books, 1982).

Terra (Newcastle upon Tyne: Bloodaxe Books, 1986).

A Book of Chinese Whispers (Newcastle upon Tyne: Bloodaxe Books, 1987).

Wormwood (Newcastle upon Tyne: Bloodaxe Books, 1987).

The heart, the border (Newcastle upon Tyne: Bloodaxe Books, 1990).

Tender to the Queen of Spain (Newcastle upon Tyne: Bloodaxe Books, 1993).

Wild Root (Newcastle upon Tyne: Bloodaxe Books, 1998).

Wire through the Heart (Budapest: Ister, 2001)

Shed: Poems 1980-2001 (Tarset: Bloodaxe Books, 2002).

You Again: Last Poems & Other Words (Tarset: Bloodaxe Books, 2004).

NON FICTION

Inside Time, with Dave Wait (London: Harrap, 1989; Mandarin, 1990).

Berlin: Coming in from the Cold (London: Hamish Hamilton, 1990; Penguin, 1991).

ANTHOLOGIES

Klaonica: poems for Bosnia, with Judi Benson (Newcastle upon Tyne: Bloodaxe Books, 1993; with *The Independent*).

Beyond Bedlam, with Matthew Sweeney (London: Anvil Press, 1997).

MAJOR ESSAYS ON KEN SMITH'S WORK

Sean O'Brien: 'Ken Smith: I Am Always Lost in It', in *The Deregulated Muse: Essays on Contemporary British & Irish Poetry* (Newcastle upon Tyne: Bloodaxe Books, 1998).

Stan Smith: 'Salvaged from the Ruins: Ken Smith's Consellations', in *British Poetry from the 1950s to the 1990s: Politics and Art*, ed. Gary Day & Brian Docherty (Basingstoke: Macmillan, 1997).

Reading from The Book of Chinese Whispers (1987)

OTHER WORDS

Ken Smith etc

I was born on 4th December 1938 in the village of Rudston, East Yorkshire, though in fact my birth certificate says I was born in the hamlet at one end of that village, a few houses known as Low Kaythorpe. Also there was a farm, a manor house with vast gardens, an army camp hidden in the woods from the bombers, and a churchyard that contained an ancient stone monolith. I remember a neighbour who grew and cured his own tobacco and kept a ferret that bit me once. I remember the bite and being told that that's what happened to people who were too curious. My father was a farm labourer, a stockman, whose problem was his inability to be servile. As a result we lived in many places, most of them isolated farms in the East, North and West Ridings, moving from farm to farm and I moving from school to school. This may have something to do with why my accent is so shifty; there is no one place I can say I came from. After a few months in Worcester I am beginning to discover Yankee intonations in my speech.

The end of all that wandering came when we settled in Hull, back in the East Riding. The horizon became either the sea (Hull is a port), or 19th-century brick, factory and housing, slum streets. Whatever I learned in school had to be tested in the street, where I learned perhaps more. That's when I began writing, in adolescence trying to bring back the rural world I was born to, finding years later that it didn't exist as I remembered it – and if it did, I didn't belong there either. The ancient village life was vanishing, and I could no more endure its structure than my father could.

I was drafted into the RAF for two years and then did what other English working-class kids did who could make the break from town and family: I became a student, courtesy of the 1944 Education Act and a state grant, at Leeds. I wrote then, but didn't think of myself as a poet. I learned, in part from two poets who were at Leeds, Jon Silkin and Geoffrey Hill, that being a poet is a matter of growth, a way of living, integral. What else I learned, then and since, in Yorkshire and Devon and Pennsylvania, should be new to no one: that we're alone mostly, that we're temporary and only we think we're important, that we're mostly accidental and at best incidental to where we are, that we may travel away from our roots in trying to discover them, that the discovery of pattern and of what endures in nature is reassuring and humbling. I think of myself as creating by writing, out of chagrin and sometimes rage attempting a more inhabitable world. Such a world for me consists of the experience of others as well as my own, and the poetry of others as it moves and helps me, a continuing revelation. I mention these things because they are important and sufficient: a few friends, books and music, solitude and its places, objects, awe, my life's images, a woman I married, three children, their lives. There is no precedence in the order. But it excludes much human activity that is to me irrelevant: all that is dedicated solely to staying alive, without questioning its meaning.

If I have anything portentous to say about poetry it is that for me the world is made real by it and value found through it, not something to be added to a drab world but integral to it, the evocation of its brilliant suffering and the vision of a world made over from this one. Without some way to cherish life through our own experience we can't assign value anywhere. I think poetry by its nature is subversive of established order, which only deadens; before it a poet can only choose between misanthropy and opposition, so he speaks from somewhere between silence and rage. So I am a propagandist: I want others to see, I want loneliness to end, and want a decent society where vision and growth are commonplace. For all the taxes they take the governments give back troops and police and corruptible officials; as a poet my job is to see that and more than that. I have tried to set the images of my life together for their own sakes, not by pelting them at the monolith but by shaping them into a larger thing, the work. Such an act by its nature is against death: the stone may he moved but I won't wait for it. But it's a longish detour. Blake said it: the way towards innocence again lies through experience. This fool will persist in his folly.

[1972]

Ken Smith comments...

Over the years my work has developed in response to the different environments in which I have arrived as much as to travel and the spaces between; mine are portable roots, some in Yorkshire, some in America, some in Devon, some now in London. Exeter, the city I most lived in, provided me with the figure of *The Wanderer* from the Anglo-Saxon *Exeter Book*; I have identified as much with him and his homelessness as with the irony of his poem having had in the cathedral library a home for the past 900 years. Writing is for me the act of discovering roots and pasts behind the present I find myself in, as if by some marvellous accident; I am located in the work I do and in the daily rediscovery of language, the magic liquid that connects me to all else. I live in that as much as anywhere. Devon also made available to me the ancient silences of Dartmoor, that marvellous museum of all that has happened to us: a museum I do not encourage anyone to visit. By Kestor, above Chagford, among the stoney leavings of the iron makers, is where I go whenever I have a decision to make, and there I feel the strongest root into the sullen past. On other days I am gregarious, and have moved recently closer and closer to dramatic expression. Community, environment, and all the minutiae of gesture and inflexion – these are all my concerns still.

Themes: environment (hence nature), domestic, human relations and human attitudes, the rural in conflict with the urban, our subjective world implanted in an indifferent objectivity. Usual verse forms – free, intuitively worked, organic. General sources – any – many accidental and incidental, but environment and history, the sense of being alive, etc. Literary sources – many and scattered, too many to mention but mostly 20th-century.

Among other things, I want to express the way we live, and comment on it: the way we live in society, the way our environment is and we with it, how we form community – the minute ways in which the shapes of our lives are expressed in habits, gestures, buildings, our conscious and unconscious reactions to weather, landscape, each other – how we bind our lives down to the smallest detail distinguishing individual or community. So in this sense I am interested in custom, and in speech, and so in language, and so in process. The poem itself is a process more than a product of this interest. I want a language that enacts and makes living, that is living rather than merely representative: a language metaphoric in itself.

[1991]

My Father's Bomb

What I'm after is only moments long: the cobbles of a farmyard in the north of England, somewhere on the Plain of York, the latter part of 1943. It is a large swept square, sheltered on all four sides by farmhouse, our tied cottage, barns, sheds, a gateway in from the road at one corner, at its diagonal another into the paddock, wherein cows, old bathtub water-trough, a great hollow willow tree, then beyond more trees, and with increasing vagueness: the village, fields, more farms, woods, towns, the world, which is at war with itself. The weather's intermittent, balmy, the square sunlit, still, to one side perhaps a few sacks, a ladder, a rake, a roller, and there are long afternoon shadows of eaves and chimneys across it all, an overhanging apple tree. The buildings are brick and ivy covered, the farmhouse painted yellow with a lurid green trim, cheap government paint, black market or plain pinched. The air is hot, dusty, still, and from the inactivity the harvest must be in, and this is perhaps the first day's rest for everyone around the yard. Perhaps it is a holiday, though there is no sense of celebration. People gather in small groups, some aloof from each other, the farmhands smoking or dozing in the late sunlight, the Italian prisoners in the barn's shadow. Most of the sounds are birds: crows in the high woods above the house, pigeons, swifts. In the square's centre, more or less, a hand pump above a well, a stone horse-trough, and to one side three or four stone steps leading nowhere forming a mounting-block. It is a farm worked by men and horses, its layout around the foldyard the style of a Roman villa. From its ambience it is not yet milking time in a late summer season: the shadows lengthening, the guests departing. Perhaps it is around five.

With hindsight I can date the scene; from my memory of the season and from the evidence of history it is sometime after September 8th, when the Allies had announced their armistice with Marshal Badoglio at Cassibile, in Sicily, seven days earlier. Thereafter the Italians were no longer prisoners, and slept in the barn. With hindsight it is an updated Brueghel, but that has nothing to do with the moment as it was, is. What I'm after was then, before memory: a long hot summer with wind in the trees, and the war going on, and all fading backwards into images of battle that are black and white newsreels that begin with a cock's crow and continue in a brisk voice describing the war in the deserts and on the seas and in the air.

But the farmyard is in full colour: the grey cobbles and dust of the yard, green of grass and ivy and moss, old red and mauve of brick and tile, clear blue of the sky, with clouds. What I want is the quality of the light around events that day of rare rural idleness, but I am already beginning to supplement memory with invention; what was is one thing, and all but irrecoverable; what I remember is another scenario, and both are separate from each other as each is from what I want, now, to make of this memory, that can only turn into the sad falsehood of a story. In reality the mounting-block stands further from the pump. In truth there may have been no apple tree, no rake, no roller, yet though the ladder is an imaginary ladder it is leaning on a real barn, and casts a real shadow. I'd like to think a radio played music through an open window, though I suspect the interlude passed without accompaniment. There is, perhaps, the dog sleeping in the shadow of the porch, there are perhaps chickens and farm cats. So much that we recall is touched by what has happened since, and already, by calling it a moment, I have opened the space in which to make a fiction, when all I wanted was to remember it as I saw it, then.

In any case the impression of stillness is false, for there are people moving, lazily as befits the hour and the season. In my mind's eye I guess there are some 20 or so around the square, in various postures between talking and silence: about a dozen Italians along the barn's side, the English hanging round doorways. Out in the centre of the yard, the focus of all our attentions, is my father. By the horse-trough with his homemade bomb he is lighting matches that go out in the slightest breeze, and he is beginning to mutter angrily to himself, knowing everyone is watching him. And my mother is beginning to move towards him across the cobblestones, carrying a white enamel bowl.

And that's as close as I can get to it, the moment I am hunting: a brief explosion, together with the moments leading to it and the long moments of time frozen that followed it. For the sake of that moment I must fit it in with the continuity of all other moments, and I am obliged therefore to account for it, to fix it in with time before and time since, to account for those present in the square. I am obliged at last to tell a story.

My father's bomb it would be called, wherein I'd circle the event, threading through the central instant of his bomb's going off, the sundry tales having little else to do with each other, these people who are variously together and variously apart. In their own small corner the farm manager and his wife and baby stand grouped to one side, aloof, superior, there to keep an eye on things. Away from them along the back porch of our next door house lean and sit several neighbours, visitors and farm hands, lads too young yet for the army, my friend Jake and Jake's mother and Jake's mother's friend and me, and the Italians. And in the middle of the square my father crouched by the pump cursing the matches and my mother who is calling him *a bloody fool*. Perhaps no one believes my father can make anything that works, let alone a bomb, so no one seems inclined to take shelter though all of us, in various degrees, cringe. The Italians who have been in a war are wary, and the English who have not are brave. All eyes are on my father.

My father, *who has made a bomb*, hates the manager, who is what my father calls a suckhole. The manager has sacked him. Therefore he has made a bomb, an act of defiance, a gesture of the powerless, I realise, with hindsight. All morning he had been in the outhouse dismantling shotgun cartridges, assembling powder and shot and fuse in a heavy glass ink bottle, packing and wadding. He wore a black determined look about his face, of anger; his anger was sometimes suicidal, manic, always bleak and unpredictable. He was making a bomb. As ever he did not say why, or how, or encourage anyone to join him as he worked, and I fancy that through the morning several attempts had been made to discover what he intended, and to deter him. If so, they had all failed.

For my father has fallen out with the farm manager, the suckhole, and has been sacked again, and will have to move on again, and the real reason is because the harvest is over, and with all these Italians the manager figures he can do without help he has to pay for. It's very simple. The Italians, though no longer enemy prisoners, can't go home yet, as Italy itself is in dispute and at war, and so they must stay here, and work. *They don't work, they lark about*, I hear the manager say to his wife, off to one side. He prefers German prisoners; more disciplined, hard-working, less trouble. As to the manager he has a wife and a young baby, their house stinks of baby shit and milk, the mother is big and floppy, and throws the dirty nappies into the corner, behind the couch, I think anywhere, until he gets someone, usually my mother the hired hand's missus, to wash them. I think the wife was always eating cakes and sweets. I can't be sure how much I'm exaggerating. With hindsight, I think she was having a breakdown, post-partum blues. Naturally I stayed away from her. And babies. I was six, maybe seven. I had my friend Jake, my stand-in brother.

I liked Jake, who lived with us as an evacuee. With him there was the farm with all its attics and rafters to explore, the orchard to raid, eggs to pinch, expeditions to the river and outward into the district, and the mysteries of the Italians. Though their status had changed little else had changed for them, but they now stayed on the farm instead of going back each night to a camp. They were trusted, which is to say they weren't. They dressed still in brown uniforms from which the distinguishing patches had been removed, leaving circles of a darker shade to distinguish them. They were still farm hands, longing to go home, and always hungry. That they sometimes sang we knew, and that they sometimes laughed, and certainly they wept, for we had seen Paulo weep bitter angry tears one day, as we watched him in the washhouse with the pliers, crack and eat his way through the kernels of a great pile of plum stones, the leavings of my mother's jam making. We didn't know why, but he wept for his hunger and poverty and what he took to be our contempt for it; he wept for the plums of his own country, and for its grapes and olives and cherries, and he wept for the scraps he was afforded in ours. No doubt he was right, and no doubt we had laughed at him. As unthinkingly Jake and I set the great hollow willow in the back field alight one late afternoon, coming home at twilight to find the whole village scrambling to put the fire out before the last of the Luftwaffe came over, everyone forming a chain of bucket passers from the pump to the emptying pond and the fire. We hid for a long time, Jake and I, advertising our guilt by our absence.

We betrayed every secret of our parents, I repeating all mine said of his. His mother visited him most weekends. She was in the Land Army, working elsewhere on the plain, *Driffield way*. His dad was in the Army, overseas, for a long time, *in the desert*. His mother would turn up on a Sunday in the company of a flash fellow, her "friend" (it was as if this were always said in quotation marks), who drove her over in his motorcar, and smoked little cigars. He'd drop her off and go elsewhere for the day while she visited. Later Flash would come to drive her back, sitting to take a cup of tea, not taking off his raincoat. He wore a brown trilby and conveyed he was better than the rest of us. He was a businessman, who hired out the threshing machines that came at harvest, and was not described as anybody's uncle or anyone's brother and had, I suspect, no name. Hindsight supplies the rest.

So there he stands in his raincoat and his brown hat, impatient to be off with her, to one side fiddling with his car keys. And there's Jake and his mum getting ready to say goodbye, and waiting just to see. There's the Italians along the shady side, and some giggling among the onlookers, and there's my father, lighting his fuse, and there's my mother, beginning her charge with the enamel bowl. Because everyone is looking at him, she bursts on the scene from nowhere.

And then the fuse takes, and everyone tenses. In this moment that stops and resumes the flow of all moments everything happens at once, and everyone ducks. The fuse flares into rapid life, he begins turning to run as at the same moment my mother reaches him with the white enamel bowl. In one motion she scoops water from the trough to douse the fuse, yelling at him for a lunatic, only, scrunching up her face against the explosion, she misses the fuse and catches him with the bowl across the head, and soaks him with the water. Colliding, they collapse into a tangle of arms and legs and fury. I think she cut him, and I think he bled. Then he's yelling at her, moving as if to hit her but the bomb goes off, with a great crack and a roar of flame skyward, the bowl skidding over the stones, and everyone down on their knees. And then silence: the taken for granted cawing of crows and pigeons and all the other birds suddenly hushed, the sudden rousing of the dogs.

The world stops for a long moment, wherein I now suppose everyone checks themselves for injuries and my parents briefly cease yelling at each other. And then, after what seems a very long time, down from out of the blue Sunday sky fell a pigeon, pierced through the gizzard by the old man's shot, dead on the farmyard cobbles, its chest stained by fresh blood. I recall it was difficult for everyone to account for the long distance in time between the shot and the bird's fall, as if for the longest time we all and the falling bird were suspended in the aftershock.

And then the world resumes its flow, my parents their quarrel, the Italians move rapidly to the cool of the barn, the manager and his wife to their parlour, Jake's mum with Flash in his car, other visitors leaving as the row between my parents gets into its stride, and Jake and I make ourselves scarce. Someone is no doubt already plucking the pigeon. The square is deserted. On the stones by the pump a patch of fresh blood marks where the bird fell.

My father fading out

Each time I recall him he's grown
thinner and paler, *am I*
making myself clear he shouts
from the hearthstone, already

I see almost through him
asleep at the fire, exhausted
evening by evening, his crossed feet
pink and opaque at the open oven door.

If he slams out now it will be
fainter and shake the house less,
less curl to his lip for his bosses –
Reggie Rat, Charlie Woods, Wallace Dixon.

For them he went topping and tailing
bent through the frozen turnips,
or stocking in summer pitched his fork
high in the air in blind sudden anger.

Now he fades out, the wireless
plays him to sleep, he wakes, asks news,
sees in the coals the black flag of a stranger,
dozes again, then is gone completely.

[from *The Poet Reclining*]

Nails

In my sleep I hear the hammering in the dark, as it has been now, for hours, the dull repeated thud of the coal hammer driving the long steel nails into wood, the wood splitting, and I glimpse him again, just before waking: my father's knotted upraised arms, his shirtsleeves folded back, banging his nails home.

He nailed up every door and every window on that farm. We'd been there a year, the year the war ended, a summer and a winter and a spring and now another summer over, it was that time again, with the corn in. Time to move on again.

Some of this I'm making up, at this distance: for instance the shirtsleeves, a detail impossible to verify, and I can only squeeze so much out of memory. But the nails and the hammer are true, raised up in his short tough arms, knotted with blue veins.

I am awake, in a dark room where the clock has stopped and the light bulb gone, hearing my father hammering in the night.

Where we lived was far enough from anywhere else, out on the great plain of York, in the old Danelaw, about five miles out of Thirsk on the Topcliffe Road, down another mile of track, tucked in behind trees. We had one neighbour about half a mile off, a farm run for its absent owner by Mart and Mabel and their rowdy sons. Mart, tall and gaunt, and with an ever-present dewdrop on the end of his long beaked nose, was the nearest my father ever got to having a mate. I used to follow him around, waiting for the dew-drop to fall. Beyond them was the railway line, with a sign saying this was the halfway point between Edinburgh and London, and far off in the distance was a great white horse cut into the hill's side. That's where we were, then.

My father is hammering in the night, from time to time pausing to select another nail, take a breather. His breath is short and heavy. He is sweating.

Meanwhile Fast Reggie, the farm manager, was off in town, drinking, being a big shot, chasing the landgirls. Reggie was a man always impatient to be somewhere else, who did everything quickly. Every night he rushed in straight from work, and was out again in record time, shaved and shiny in his blue suit, off down the road in the big black box Ford we called the breadbox. Other times the breadbox carried chickens to market or a sheep to the vet. My mother would time him changing. Reggie's comings and goings and the girls he sometimes sneaked in were closely observed. My mother was a woman who missed nothing. Between Reggie and my father no love was lost. They hated each other.

Not that my father was entirely innocent. Swift to anger, he would strike out, he was sometimes violent, vicious, vengeful, always moody and secretive, bearing his grudges along with him. Around the house he'd break things, slam his dinner in the fireback, roll on the floor in inarticulate fury, lock my mother out or himself in, slam off to the river muttering suicide. I was always afraid of him, though all this seemed to be quite normal. Sometime that summer, on a Sunday with Reggie out for the day, he'd got carried away burning rubbish too near the cornstacks, and almost set the lot ablaze. We fought all afternoon to put the fire out, damp it down. He got away with that. He was always tinkering with something, always curious.

But now he was sacked again. There'd been some row between him and Reggie. Reggie had called the police, there had been violence offered. I watched them from the cool of the barn as they sorted it out and decided there was nothing they could do. Perhaps there was a real reason, but for my father it was only that the season was over, and the farm wouldn't need him through the winter, and we were on a week's notice, and on the move again. The war was over, and the cheap labour of prisoners of war was being replaced by incoming DPs, strangers who would take any wage, who knew hunger worse than ours. We were on the road again. Every time that happened, a grim mood overcame both of them. He wouldn't be bested, as he'd say. *I have a handle to my name.* And he'd get his own back.

But Fast Reggie was gone to town, and he'd locked, padlocked, bolted from the inside, roped up, jammed and otherwise blocked every entrance to the farm. This being the country, and we dependent on the farm for everything, this meant no supper. No eggs, no milk, no hastily strangled chicken.

My father mutters in my half sleep, half waking. He'd not be bested. In the twilight I see him sitting on the cobbles, grumbling with Mart and his sons, ancient tribesmen considering how best to maintain their honour. It seems to take a long time, this muttering and cursing and consideration of the ways of revenge, it is a long pause before action. I can imagine now, the gleam of the dewdrop on the end of Mart's nose in the light of the oil lamp from the kitchen window as they get up at last, excited now they have resolved what to do. If they can't get in, no one else will. They'll nail the place up. Mart squeezes out his rollup, puts the butt back in his tin. Mart's sons go off to get the box of 12-inch nails and the hammers, and my father goes to the coalhouse for the coal hammer, wanting to get on with it. I'm sent to the lane, to watch out for the lights of Reggie's returning breadbox. And then, in the dark, for hours, by the light of storm lamps and torches, they nailed up the farm: sties, byres, stores, sheds, outbuildings, and the great barn into which I recall some months before my mother bursting, waving a Union Jack: the war was over. We'd won. The German POWs sat down together, in absolute silence. They'd lost.

In the morning of course he knew nothing, did he, though the Police were called again and went off shrugging their shoulders. He had heard nothing, nor any of us, the matter having nothing to do with us. We didn't work there any more. Meanwhile the cows needed milking, the calves and pigs feeding, and the farm must be gotten into somehow, and soon it was Fast Reggie's turn to fetch the coal hammer and break his way in. In the end he had to replace every door and window, and its jambes.

My father stirs in the dark, tapping the nails in gently at first, then standing back and thumping them in. In the half light he is sweating, his face creased in a fury, his eyes fixed only on what he is doing. My father is nailing himself out.

Being the third song of Urias

Lives ago, years past generations
perhaps nowhere I dreamed it:
the foggy ploughland of wind
and hoofprints, my father
off in the mist topping beets.

Where I was eight, I knew nothing,
the world a cold winter light
on half a dozen fields, then
all the winking blether of stars.

Before like a fool I began
explaining the key in its lost locked box
adding words to the words to the sum
that never works out.

                Where I was
distracted again by the lapwing,
the damp morning air of my father's
gregarious plainchant cursing
all that his masters deserved
and had paid for.
             Sure I was
then for the world's mere being
in the white rime on weeds

among the wet hawthorn berries
at the field's edge darkened by frost,
and none of these damned words to say it.

I began trailing out there in voices,
friends, women, my children,
my father's tetherless anger, some
like him who are dead who are
part of the rain now.

[from *The Poet Reclining*]

Fun City

Where I was born, or near enough, was called 'the seaside': the place I've named Fun City. Brisk and windy, it sits on the North Sea coastline of England, the modest centrepiece of the bay of its own name, in what was once called the East Riding but is now North Humberside. Around there people put a sign in their windows: 'If I'd wanted to change my address I'd have moved.'

I recall: hot jugs of tea on the beach, sandcastles and sandwiches, Punch and Judy, the old man unwinding, taking off his shoes. Maybe there were donkeys, or maybe that was later, or elsewhere. I remember a band, a parade of sailors, the evening walk along the harbour's north pier, an ice cream if you were lucky and if you'd been good, pocket money for the amusements. And in there slot machines, penny rolls, dodgems, the laughing sailor in his glass boat, drunk as ever. My recall is as dotty as anyone's – as particular, as general, as odd, as accurate and as misremembered. I was small and surprised by everything: the row of harlequin clown faces moving slowly side to side in synch with each other, their open mouths waiting at the rollerball stands, their perfect strangeness.

And always the bay mouth, the sea like a great snail, and along the front the rockshop and the great twists of candy, and the beach and the streets busy and crowded. Back then, in my first dim memory, there were great tangles of barbed wire along the tidemark. We dug or dozed in deckchairs behind this. It had to do with the war, the grown-ups said, just as everything else had to do with the war. They talked of other days, of swimming and walking in all that water, and they seemed to hint such things would be possible again, and they used that other phrase of theirs: 'when the war's over'. Meanwhile there were mines and shrapnel and enemy ships over the horizon and U-boats under the surface, and many things unseen. We were at war, and that seemed natural to me, a condition I'd been born to, and the condition of the world as I understood it then if I understood it at all. Years later 'peace' was the more unusual idea to get used to. For me, at four, there were as there are for any child, many things not possible. I guess I assumed that paddling in the sea and the removal of wire and the end of the war, however connected, were amongst the things that would come about when I was old enough. And that, somehow or other, would happen in its own time.

Meanwhile in the great meanwhile, the town was shelled from offshore, and many killed. In the village where we lived soldiers rushed to learn their trades, camped out in the woods, using the main road for their drill square. Planes suddenly came burning out of the sky, at night the searchlights crisscrossed south towards Hull, and the distant boom of bombs falling there came to us through the nights. Sometimes we went there, my mother and I visiting her father; that is to say, we went on holiday to a city under the Blitz, and spent each night sitting out in my grandfather's concrete shelter in the garden, the landscape heaving beneath our feet. And there my grandfather, home at last from the sea, told his tales of distant places and shipwrecks, pausing only for the whistle of a close one, his finger raised, checking how close the bomb would fall. 'That's not for us,' he'd say. 'It doesn't have our name on it.'

Peace came. Peace went. Three years into the war we moved, first to Sunk Island on the grey north edge of the Humber, then further inland. The 'we' of it were a farm labourer, his wife, their son, yours truly, and when I was six, my sister. For years we wandered from farm to farm, tied house to tied house, across the Ridings. And always there were returns to Fun City, mostly in what summers we had. In some upland village the Scouts or the Choir or the W.I. or the Mothers' Union or the village pub would get a trip up, saved for and the bus booked months ahead.

There were other seasides: Scarborough, Whitby and Robin Hood's Bay, and on the other side Blackpool and Morecambe. Always there was an early start, a long trip overland, games with I-Spy and number plates and white horses, crisps and sandwiches and beer bottles opened early, and the waiting for the one moment, to be first to glimpse across land suddenly foreshortened: the flat grey belly of the sea.

In other years, maybe when there'd been overtime, we spent a whole week in Fun City, in bed and breakfast. Day after day the sand stretched to the white cliffs, boats came and went in the harbour mouth and ships lay halfway over the horizon, and the sea basked. And when my grandfather retired here where he now lies in his own 6 foot of chalky loam, there were visits to him. With his second wife whom all my family loathed all their days together he lived in the house my mother now lives in, where I now visit her with increasing frequency.

She ages. The town declines. And I digress though from what I don't know. My invisible thread here is a continuity of visiting the same place over 40 years, noting its changes through the foggy in-accuracies of memory, some of it childhood's perceptions. Grown older, I can no longer tell what's changed in the world and what's changed in me, and how much of my recall is biased. I think the town, like all of us having lost its purpose, can't find another.

The last coal boat, the *Blue Billy*, came and went in about 1903, the brick and fertiliser deliveries fell off, and the place was no longer a port. It still has the fishing. It still has the railway, though not in winter. For years it got by on holidaymakers and day trippers; they come back in fewer numbers, some, affluent, to further fields, and some – poorer – not at all. Hotels converted to self-service flats, and fast food moved in. The beach has thinned. Fun City is like elsewhere, scratching its civic head thinking how to attract more visitors.

And like elsewhere the collective head, having been scratched, decided to rip out the floral clock and the miniature golf course in favour of high intensity entertainment. Now, along the seaward side of the town centre from the harbour north – 'the front' – are roundabouts and wings and noisome machineries. High intensity fun bawls out its lonesomeness across the harbour piers, in a punctuation of gull cries, and the generators roar, the Spider and Rollercoaster turn, and from the House of Horrors comes the cackle of taped laughter, infecting with its hysteria the half dozen punks and skins sitting round the dodgems.

Bingo glitter spreads along the shop-fronts, neons flashing on/off. And by the path along the front, at intervals, clear plastic boxes of egg shaped bubblegum prizes that cackle from time to time, like demented chickens. The silicon chip in an imitation parrot squawks, its tail flicks, and we agree how lifelike. In the bars the disco music flashes, and video machines chatter.

No one seems much pleased by any of this.

Family group

He also was a stormy day: a squat mountain man
smelling of sheep and the high pasture, stumping
through pinewoods, hunched and small, feeling
the weather on him. Work angled him.
Fingers were crooked with frost, stiffened.

Ploughing he would fix his eye on the hawthorn,
walking firm-booted, concerned for the furrow.
Horse and man in motion together, deliberate,
one foot put before the other, treading cut clay.
He would not see the bird perched on the plough.
He would not chase the plover limping over stubble.

He was my father who brought in wood and lit
the hissing lamp. And he would sit, quiet
as moor before the fire. She drew him
slowly out of silence. She had a coat
made from a blanket and wore boys' shoes.
She was small and had red hands, firm-boned,
and her hair was greying. The house was stone
and slate. It was her house, his home,
and their family, and they quarrelled often.

She churned butter, baked, and scrubbed floors,
and for forty years he laboured the raw earth
and rough weather. In winter we made mats
from rags with pegs. We guarded ourselves
and were close. We were poor and poorer banking
each pound saved. Each year passed slowly.

Now he lives in the glass world of his shop,
and time is grudged. Ham and tinned meat
and vegetables are his breathing day.
He works harder and is unhappy. She too
stoops through the labouring year, is greyer
and grumbles. Nothing gets made any more
but money that cannot be made. Nothing
means happiness. The light comes down wires,
water through tubes. All is expensive, paid.

Silence is gone from their lives, the city
has taken that poised energy. Violence
is articulate. The deliberate motion is gone
and he moves with pain through time that is work
that is cash. He will not notice the crashed
gull fallen in the storm, the grabbing sparrows.
She cannot ease him into speech, or be content
before the broody fire. She is in fashion now.
But seasons pass them without touching.
They will not feel the winter when it comes.

[from *The Poet Reclining*]

Valley

Pale grass
a long flag
striped once by the river,
the one
wandering blue star
of the heron.

In the light's early silence
the farmers crank the old box Ford
full of chickens. The cock croaks,
he has counted his wives,
some are missing,
plucked and stiffening
under the market awning. Nothing else
but a pheasant's stuttering,
a distant bell sound. I see
in the starry river
the keel mark.

Tightened into the bank's
wooded side under the steep
hill's stone shadow
a Viking boat
is still vanishing.

[from *The Poet Reclining*]

Comment from an interview:

The poem 'Valley' is about a particular valley in Yorkshire. I lived a
couple of years there, and when I left at about aged ten I continued
to think of myself in that landscape. In some ways I thought of it
as *my* valley. It was bleak upland, a place of solitude, where in the
absence of mates I invented characters, made up stories and dialogue,
and went about talking aloud to myself. I began to be a writer
there. When I moved to the city I thought more and more of this
valley, and once I went back there, as an adult. I found it wasn't
much as I remembered, and wasn't at all a place I wanted to live.
It wasn't *mine*. Over the years I wrote about this place, and my
feelings for its loss. But what was lost was childhood itself, and

writing about it was a lament. Eventually when I suppose I had exorcised this feeling through several poems, I wrote this last poem, 'Valley', as a sort of farewell. The place had become distant to me, almost two-dimensional, and so the poem begins with a sort of map, with a flat thing like a flag.

So I began with a design for a flag for this lost country. The flag would be green of course, for the pale green of its thin upland grass. And there would be one stripe through it, white I suppose, for the river running through. And then there would be a star, which would be a smoky sort of blue, and because the star represented herons I used to watch for hours there, it would be a star that would move around the flag mysteriously, now here and now there, as herons do. So then I had three images, and when I put them together I had a line or so: *pale grass a long flag striped once by the river, and the one wandering blue star of the heron.*

I had a description of my flag and a reminder of the valley and a beginning to my poem. I could say this phrase over and over to myself, aloud or in my head, like a bit of music or a loop of imaginary film in which the camera panned across the valley and river and closed on the figure of a heron, and then dissolved into the flag I'd made. I had something to remember the place by, to store it in my memory or lull myself to sleep with. I could write down the phrase in various ways. I could play with it. It might not have become the beginning of a poem, but through repeating it I began to glimpse the other possibilities and images of the rest of the poem. So far this is only a description of the beginning.

In a workshop this step by step demonstration points to mundane beginnings not in an idea or a desire to write a poem so much as in an image, a phrase, a scrap of rhyme perhaps, a sequence of thought, a mnemonic. To begin here is to begin with something like play or song or dance, though it may not help to call it such, nor, for that matter, to call it poetry. What's to be avoided here is the inhibitedness of the self-conscious act involved in thinking *I'm writing a poem*; with schoolchildren this reflex may block the flow rather than release it. But here, in explanation, I can say the star on the flag reminds me of the heron, is associated in my mind with it. [...]

Bringing these images together we are then talking of *association*, the personal and often idiosyncratic means by which we associate one image or word or idea or mood with another, and setting these images in the context of each other I'm describing a constellation of associations, images, words, that became the poem.

Playing field observations

In the light before rain
counting the hard little
yellows of the dayseyes I went
down the sea-opened valley –

a neat country it's said
of parkland and flood plain
squared like the blind man's garden
between the waters.

Sang goodbye to the elms,
glimpsed by the canal
blue smokey lift of a heron,
accepting my birthday.

How the shadows move in
at such news and are strange
in the light. This feather
left for his marker my brother

the crow had dropped by the goalpost
seems a dead man's finger
keeping his page
in the unfinished biography.

[from *The Poet Reclining*]

Unpublished commentary:

I had been for a walk in a place I often walked, years ago when I
wrote this poem, in a town I used to live in. Neruda says: *if you
want to learn to be a poet you must first learn to walk*. It happens I
like walking. Usually I find things, and with the rhythm of it I
can think, and walking alone is best: the thought doesn't have to
be shared while you're thinking it. More chance of thinking some-
thing out. Less chance of interruption.

On this particular day I guess I was feeling moody. The walk
took me through open country towards the sea, though I did not
go as far, through the old flood plain of a river, which is to one
side. To the other is a canal, the first pound lock in England, and

there are trees and bits of real country, fields, hedgebacks and what were once called watermeads. Back then Dutch Elm disease had condemned the elms to the chainsaw, and maybe I was feeling sad for that. No more elm trees. The place is mostly playing fields. I guess I like nature more natural. Again, the place, the scenery, becomes the occasion for some thoughts, mostly gloomy, to do with growing older, with knowing we must die. I'd thought about my grandfather, who'd not long before that died of a heart attack, sitting in his chair with his pipe in his mouth and his forefinger keeping the page he'd reached in a book he was reading, closed in his lap where he'd nodded off, and died in his sleep.

With these sorts of thoughts in my head I came home. They weren't all gloomy; in that particularily sharp light just before rain where everything stands out sharply I'd noticed many details, amongst them the dayseyes in the grass, which get in as representatives of all I'd enjoyed seeing. And I'd watched a heron, for a long time, as he stood so still I'd taken him first for a broken stump. Watching herons is tricky, they're so still, and sooner or later you'll look away, and it's that moment they'll suddenly take off, perhaps to vanish, perhaps to stand just as still somewhere else. This time I'd caught him as in one sudden movement he broke into flight. *Like smoke* I'd thought. And by one of the goalposts I'd picked up a crow feather.

I think it was the crow feather that started it. I think its Victorian widow-weed colours worked as images work, immediately suggesting the topic *death*. Black, we say on this part of the planet, is the colour of death. Everyone knows that. And anyway here were the dead elm trees, and here was the wild raggedy country being rollered into playing fields, so there was my topic that day. But note how the image works: watch the feather. As for the parkland (people said how 'neat' it was now) that made me think of the blind man who lived next door to my grandfather, which set me thinking about him, but again, let's watch the image. The blind man's garden is what a blind man would design, plants not for their flowers but for their scents and sounds and touch, and the whole of it designed in squares so that he could get about it with his cane. I liked the garden, didn't much like the parkland.

So here I had two working images: the crow feather, the blind man's garden, images that underlie an idea because they gave rise to it, metaphors that transfer thinking and feeling from one thing to another: they move things along. The other images were of the place: the elms, the heron, the daisies in the grass. Otherwise I must have had some words in my head, but I don't know which they were now. I think they are to do with the shadows moving in the minute you're having a good time. More likely what I had was a sense of the mood I was in, a moodiness transferred to the place with its wind and marshy bits of pasture, and more likely perhaps a rhythm in my head of what the sounds of whatever the words would be. Mostly the words were blanks. It's probably more like doing algebra than writing. I had what we call a constellation of images (crow, heron, tree, blind man, dead man), a sense of a mood, a few words, mostly blanks. I decided to begin by merely saying where I'd been, in a very general way, because the details or when and where are really irrelevant. That got me started, with the daisies, and I used the old spelling because I wanted to emphasise how they seemed to me: *eyes of the day*. That observation led me to the next and immediate comment in the second stanza, and I'd made my move on the blind man's garden image. The analogy. Somewhere about there, returning to simply saying what I'd seen, brought back the heron, and then I think I didn't know where to go. I needed something to hang these things on, this observation and that reflection, and around there I must have decided that the poem was about growing older and accepting it, and here I told a lie. It wasn't my birthday, but then it might have been, and these such thoughts as having a birthday might provoke, and what difference would it make? Who would know? We call this poetic licence.

Having introduced this fiction, the poem could then proceed. I moved the shadows in, and brought in the crow feather with all its implications, and used the visual similarity of the feather and the finger to bang it all home, and didn't mention that I was thinking about my grandfather. I didn't want the poem to be that personal, but more universal, and anyway the poem was about how I felt about dying and growing older, about change and decay.

The rest was working with the words, listening to them, trying out their rhythms, turning them this way and that, in a long line and a short, in couplets and three line and four line stanzas and in one big lump, slapping the poem around sometimes like a piece of pastry or clay, and there were other words before I found the words I wanted, or the ones I finally settled for, which are here. The title took forever, and still doesn't please me. Perhaps I was uncertain what the poem was trying to be about. With all the babble all around and all the other babble in our heads it's difficult to separate out one string in all the tangle. But walking helps.

The writer's trade: FROM 'Departure's speech'

Words like rain in the applemint. In my trade
I'm a journeyman living the life of waste nothing,
odds picked in skips, scraps my dead father kept,
all the words I can steal so look out for yourself,
my sisters, my brothers. I'm Thief, Joker, Twister,
Departure the weathergrained theatrical beached
at the Colony more often than not weeping in whisky
muttering *stagecoach, vulva, rain in the applemint,*
anarchist-in-waiting to the republic of survival.
For instance I might say *dry white Chablis pray*
and the barmaid reply *we've only dry roasted.*

[from *Ignore Previous Telegram* (from *Terra*), reprinted in *Shed*]

Invisible Thread [# 2]

Mexico, she said, with the brilliant light. And when I got there
what I'd always wanted to see: an iguana. But when I saw one it
was dead, slung across the shoulder of a one-eyed man. And I
hadn't taken my camera.

Taunton, Bridgewater, Weston-super-Mare. White gulls against the
looming rain, and in the flat drained fields of further Somerset the
pollards in early morning light. All this to say where we are assorted
passengers and strangers passing time on a train north past Brunel's
bridge and Bristol's tall terraces: the woman I shall call The Peacock
Lady, her companion The Grey Man. The inevitable question.

So what do you do?

I reply. If only doing so didn't conjure up so many daft notions
from the glamour industry about *the writer*. The Grey Man is sus-
picious. He doesn't think that listening and looking and travelling the
earth on any frail excuse, then plundering and writing down the
words of others is *work*. He doesn't think that being self-employed
and living across the river, as the taxman describes my trade, is *work*.

So how do you become a writer? asks The Peacock Lady, meaning:
how do you work? The three feathers in her hat nod as she talks.
The Grey Man stares beyond her into fields. Tell me about Mexico,
I say. And the iguana. You look at everything. You suspend com-
ment, in the first place. You note gesture and detail, you train the
ear to listen and the eye to look. You train your memory to recall,

for example, a woman in a pink hat with three peacock feathers talking about her holiday in Mexico. You listen. You do not interrupt, and then you make, if you can, some use of the event. She describes the lake of still water, and the three men walking down the path towards her, one carrying a fish, another dragging a snake, and the third the one-eyed man, carrying the iguana. In Spanish sign-talk he describes killing the iguana, and how they will cook it. She describes their laughter, the mountains beyond them, the blue sky brilliantly empty after the downpour. You describe her. Is my reply.

But she hadn't taken her camera. She has no picture of the event, she says. But she has she has, I shout silently to the waiting passengers at Bristol Temple Meads. Language, I mutter on the long curve beyond Bristol Parkway, is pictures, pictures of events. Pictures and sounds. Images and rhythms. What people say. Look at the pictures, I nod to Gloucestershire. Listen to them.

What else is advice on how to do it for those who want passionately to be writers; warnings, moans in the dark, groans off. It's an uphill trade. Publishers grow fewer, their products more coffee-table ephemera, their decisions made oftener by accountants than by editors; they're not, despite the propaganda, hunting hard for new talent. Despite rejection slips, you keep going: listening, remembering, writing down. Then rearrange, edit, select, invent, add, imagining e.g. that there ever was a woman sitting on a train through Bristol and beyond, who talked of Mexico and iguanas, and how she hadn't taken her camera, and didn't realise the words she used were camera enough. Give her a pink hat, or a crocodile handbag, and a companion called the Grey Man.

Take The Grey Man.

Item: he's a librarian. Tell him it's fine for him to lend out a writer's books to the public free gratis and for nothing, and fine for the public too. The writer has a royalty, of course, usually 10% of purchase price of the one copy loaned many times. Nothing more. And while you're glad when people read your work, you'd like to make a living. Everyone else, including librarians, expects to do so. […]

Item: decide he's a taxman. Tell him, now the Inland Revenue are offering to tax awards and grants to writers, that you protest; such awards are honours, often made for research or for travel, for work done or in hand, but often enough in lean years the only corn to feed the chickens with. Tell the Grey Man.

Tell him about The Peacock Lady. And the iguanas.

[1978]

77

CLAIRE McNAMEE

Some notes on the Uncertainty Principle: 'The wanderer Yacob'

Over the years I've come to recognise the figure of the wanderer, under various guises, speaking through most of what I've written. When I came to write this work I had already decided to just get on with it, to write directly about the archetype, the character of the wanderer, and these are merely some notes about him.

In all ages and at all times in so far as I can tell in most places there's the wanderer. Usually he's male, or a male figure, and since I'm a male writer, my available viewpoints concur with his. For some reason, he's outside established social groupings, and because for some reason he once was in them (the family, the neighbourhood, the kinship group, the gang) but now is no longer, he therefore speaks to what he can no longer join or return to. It does not matter why: he is an exile in one sense or another, whether because he is in his original group considered (by their lights) a crook or crazy, whether his role is as prophet or fortune teller, troubadour or poet, bartender or soldier of fortune, this does not matter. He is an outsider, and an outsider's function to society is in his facility for insight. He is a critic, if only for having had different, and varied, experience in other (or on the periphery of other) groupings. Standards of goodness or beauty or acceptable social behaviour may differ elsewhere. He knows, as those who have never been outside their cultural space do not, that there are no absolute standards. He knows that time and place and context change the rules, and while he may adopt certain guidelines for behaviour (his own, others') he knows there are no circumstances when any rule may not merely be violated, but dropped.

Hence the uncertainty principle. Nothing is certain; not rules that can be simply broken, nor norms nor priorities that cannot be changed. Some may be more fixed than others.

When Heisenberg posited the Uncertainty Principle he did far more than close off simple physical certainty about observations made of the subatomic world. In effect he was speaking of the limitations of human perception, and by acknowledgement, the limitations of human thought. There are two ways to observe, for instance, an electron. One involves an electron microscope through which at one end the human eye at the other observes the electron as a fixed entity – a particle that, while it is moving, is nevertheless a thing moving in space. The camera records the electron through the microscope as a fixed point, as matter. The other way to look at the electron is with a laser, which observes not the fixed point but the movement made, and the result to observation or on film is a wave, or the line of it. Through the laser, the electon is energy. Through the microscope, however, it is matter.

And these two, matter and energy, the moving wave and the fixed point, are opposites of each other.

And here all the Ancient Greeks wake to object. Socrates reminds us that he said, quite clearly, a thing cannot both be itself and its opposite. It must be one or the other. This is the foundation of all thought, and of all science, and the first and last assumptions of all observation. Of our perceptions. There are other possibilities: that the microscope is dirty, that the eye of the beholder is cloudy, or that the perceiver is unreliable; 'mad' we would say. Socrates acknowledges as well that some things are not explicable once we apply whatever rules we have, in this case the rules of words. He holds up three fingers of one hand, and points to the middle finger, *large* compared with the index or the pinky or the ring finger, and therefore in all case large, just as the pinky is in all cases *small*. But in another contest the ring finger is compared with the pinky, small compared with the middle finger, and therefore can be described only as x or y in comparison, in context, requiring an extension of the sentence.

The observations of Heisenberg and Niels Bohr do not depend on this sort of context, but on the context (in the case of the electron) of how the electron is perceived. Whatever is there as the perceived electron behaves according to the rules we ourselves have deduced both as matter and as energy, yet our logic, and our language, tells us it cannot behave (and therefore be) both. The classical logic of the Greeks, the Aristolelian logic of geography and mathematics, its descent through Imperial and Catholic Rome, and all its attendant influence on our thinking, on our education systems whether medieval or modern, on the very language we use to express thought, is thereby broken. Here is a thing that is both itself and its opposite, and that is there whether we observe it or not, and the problem if there is one is of our observing it. The problem lies both in our need to perceive, and in our biased perception.

And on the personal level we know that so much we thought to be true turns out not to be, or at any rate to have been dependent on the imperfections of our perception of events at the time, the unreliability of report, the tricks of even our own memories, the different emphases on what words mean. Rapid developments within technology within our own lifetimes, and all their attendant social upheavals, merely confuse us. We find our perceptions are all we have, and that our perceptions are unreliable. So what do we know?

We have come, therefore, to the end of certainty about anything, a situation that includes uncertainty and disagreement about what words mean, a place where poetics and physics and linguistics meet. It is not a good place to be, and there are always easy options, political and philosophical and religious, into which to lurch for refuge. The wanderers in my poems would always love to do this, perhaps be born again or Marxist or merely be in love or drunk or have the whole world readily described, with certainty again, just as in early childhood. They also know they cannot return, either to childhood or its adult naiveties. Their condition is merely uncertainty. They know that wherever they are when they hear the news, the news is colour for that place. And they can say read any two news accounts of the same event, etc, to demonstrate their point.

My contention is that the outsider, the wanderer, has always operated from some principle of uncertainty, and that now, as we all enter philosophical uncertainty, we are therefore all wanderers. Heisenberg's Principle simply says: the rules have changed. His theory seeks to hold together, in one concept, two opposites that are incompatible in any other theory. Put simply: there is no certainty, though you may feel it is so, unless it is this statement itself. What does not change is change itself.

For after all, as Saul Bellow asked in his Nobel acceptance speech: what the hell do we know anyway? We read it, we hear it, we stand around with highballs in our hands being assured to know, from at best secondary sources verabl or written, that this or that really happened, that the real truth is x or y. Constantly, we are challenged, rightly, to evaluate the source of the information. But all we really know directly from observation is very little, confined to our immediate environments. And even that is suspect, subject to what we want or prefer to believe, what our perceptions or memories tell us, to what of that we can get into acceptable language, to what will be told.

And so to the wanderer, as archetype. In the Anglo-Saxon *Exeter Book* there is the poem, 'The Wanderer', and its companion, 'The Seafarer'. Elsewhere there's 'Widsith', whose name describes him. Each character is a composite, I think, and I've lumped all three into one composite personality. They are so in any case for the sake of the many anonymous wandering poets who must have spoken them, developed and changed and cut their cloth to local requirements, handed them on as poems from generation to generation, misremembered, embroidered, added. And so I treat the stock character here – a sort of hydra figure with many heads and many voices.

Pound made, I thought, a pretty poor translation of the Seafarer, who is merely a wanderer by water. As a Pound poem it is interesting; as a treatment of inventive language it is interesting. But the poem in his hands never struck me as the words of a seafarer. They were always too erudite. And while for years I thought that what I wanted to do was to provide my own translation of these poems, I've never got very far with that project, and come to see it pointless. The [Michael] Alexander translations are good enough for me, side by side with the originals, which for years were available in the Cathedral library in Exeter. Even a xerox made from them was enough. At bottom I suppose it seems to be there's no point explicating the experience of an 8th-century man, 'cut off from kind', who's for whatever reason lost his kinship group. While I can empathise with his loneliness, I can't much empathise with him: what he longs for is to be part of the tribe again, in its specific function as the male war band, whose values are aggression, dominance, killing, theft, and the sharing of the loot, and whose loyalties are to his leader. By extension, his values are the yob's, or the Nazi's. The wanderer in the 20th century would I think be a recruit to the SS or the National Front. Nowhere does he mention women.

Ultimately it seemed to me a waste of energy to concentrate on this particular Wanderer by translating him, running the risk of being ensnared by his values and his personality. Whoever wrote the poem down was, I suspect, a Christian convert, a monk, who perhaps having been a wanderer had in age found himself a billet in the Church, and who therefore falsified the pagan longings in the poem. The lord of the kinship group becomes the capitalised Lord in heaven, and the outer frame of Seafarer and Wanderer forms a capsule of homily.

There is much that Pound rightly decided to leave out. And in any case what I had become interested in, within all the framing devices of the two poems, was the archetype of the wanderer himself.

Therefore I asked myself, what would the wanderer write now, in the late 20th century. I began to think of the characters of wanderers: musicians, salesmen, mercenary soldiers, bartenders, gipsies, wandering mechanics in the early industrial revolution, printers, journeymen. Perhaps originally they had begun as orphans, or exiles, or countrymen forced into the towns, or criminals. Perhaps they were as much represented by the busker on the subway as by the wandering Hasid in the Russian Pale; they followed the motorway's construction gangs just as they followed the railways; some took to the sea, some were by all standards mad. Whatever their case, they always seemed to have some independence of viewpoint. They were critical, even in silence.

And I thought, further, that beneath the lives we have lived, whether as urban and industrial inhabitants of contemporary society, or as the peasants we were for many centuries living in a fixed landscape fixed lives, there lies the fascination of the circus come to town, or of the arrival of the beggar, the pilgrim, the wandering friar bringing news from elsewhere. And back of that, deep in our memories, the fact for many more generations we were rovers, herdsmen with our cattle as the Masai are still or as the shepherds of 14th-century Montaillou were, and back before that hunters who followed the movements of the herds. And I fancied, though it may be a thought, that in the displaced wanderer figure lay this older memory, and that in him it could not be suppressed, and that because of him fixed and organised society may be changed, disrupted, or at any rate entertained where otherwise it would [b]ore itself to death.

What Eliot feared of the wandering Jew, that he introduces new ideas and therefore threatens established society, became then another prototype, and this thought led me to thinking, somehow, of Jacob. Coupled with this, and my aversion ultimately to the Anglo-Saxon wanderer in that his wandering is so womanless as to fail to mention even their absence, I found the figure of Jacob more amenable. As a result he became the main, though not the only, representative of the wandering archetype.

He leaves his family. He is obliged to, for he has stolen the blessing of his father reserved for his elder brother, by disguising himself in the skins of kids. He goes east, across the desert, to Laban the Syrian, who is his mother's kin. On the [way] he sleeps in the desert, resting his head on a stone that he later sets up as an altar to memorialise the dream he has there, a vision he would have said. He dreamed of a ladder going up to heaven, and up and down that ladder angels, working between the worlds. He is therefore a witness, perhaps an intermediary, between God and man. Thereafter he works for Laban, putting in seven years for love of Rachel, Laban's younger daughter, only at the end of his time to be fobbed off with Leah, the elder. Presumably there's been a clever use of veils and disguise (again: tit for tat, Jacob), and Laban reasons that the rules state the elder daughter must be married first, so what? Jacob accepts, and works another seven years for Rachel. He is expressing a preference, for one over the other. There must be passion here then, for Rachel. Therefore we have love, and feeling.

Later, married to the both of them, begetting children left and right and by their handmaidens, he ingeniously cheats Laban. Rachel steals her father's household gods. In the desert Jacob wrestles with an angel. The fight goes on all night, and seems to have been an even match. In shamanistic terms, Jacob is wrestling with another power, an ally, and because he gives good account of himself compels the ally to give him something. This is presumably a knowledge that gives him greater authority, and for which he must pay. He is wounded in the thigh, and limps thereafter, perhaps from a dislocated leg joint. The sign of what he gets is a new name: *Israel*.

These are merely notes, to describe the imaginative basis of this work. The rest is speculation, and I am merely drawing on long traditions of the wanderers, present in all literatures that I have encountered, if only as the picaresque.

from The wanderer Yacob

A gambling man, dice and a fancy
Italian deck in his waistcoat.
A salesman with his patents,
survivor on his silver tongue.

Comic. Piano player. Drifter
with the railroads, poacher
of other men's work and women,
on the moon's tack, a migrant.

Or takes to the sea's roads,
a carpenter, bright tools
in a box made him shipman
twice round the world's rim.

[from *Wormwood*, reprinted in *Shed*]

War, violence and men: *Terra* (1986)

extract from Hawkwood

Seated, a man with the tools of his trade,
solitary in the company of weapons,
always the warrior, apart,
etched into metal in a moment of brooding.

Mostly he sleeps sound till first light,
by day lives the life of his time:
fighting to live he will fight
for cash money or credit. Or not fight.

At his ease when he may be,
who can never go home now,
his landscape the blunt northerly speech
glimpsed through the window to his left

where the hills are already going to sleep,
the road hatched away into more shadow
always closing round him. In the foreground
a single candle he has lit against the night.

Dark Jokes

Most of *Terra* I wrote between the summers of 1982 and 1984, much
of it on the hoof and scribbled in notebooks, and no doubt my
grainy hurry shows. By then, most of my work selected and tidily
reduced to one book 5″ x 8½″ fitting one pocket, I think I wanted
to write about immediate and pressing events, day by day. I wanted
to catch how it felt, to me at any rate, to be in whatever place (in
and around London, mostly) in the present tense. The here and now
of it having since become the then and there, history being in a
hurry, I can call that time another book in another pocket, and thank
you Mr Bloodaxe.

It wasn't my intention, therefore, to begin with a sequence about
a 14th century mercenary hawking his military skills around the
Italian states, and living in a more or less permanent condition of
readiness. But the character of Hawkwood had intrigued me as I

first came across him in Geoffrey Trease's *The Condottieri*, where he is one chapter. He seemed to me one who might have gone to Canterbury by way of Southwark, except that he had left England as a young man for the French Wars with nothing but his dead father's best horse, and came back half a century later as a funeral. He seemed familiar, a persistent Englishman, the prototype perhaps of the old soldier grown wiser and softer from his wars, with his own independent code as to honesty, integrity, loyalty, and so forth; a man who having fought, killed, suffered, seen some he loved dead, seen slaughter and been its agent, yet come out recognisably human and not yet obsolete.

Not much has changed, I think, and though the present demands constant attention, it contains the past with all its bloody roots, and the present's not so safe at all, nor disconnected. All this is serious stuff, and keeps the lads awake at night in the dorm, and dulls their lessons. No doubt it has become a preoccupation with me: the investigation of what horrifies us, despite, yet the more because of, all the beauty round us, and given the universe is a very dangerous place in any case. Through Hawkwood, as I knew him better, I was able to write about war and war-making, about violence, about men.

Something of this preoccupation, I think, led me to be writer in residence at Her Majesty's Prison Wormwood Scrubs, where I'm coming to a conclusion that the study of male violence, with all it personally and collectively inflicts, is necessary and urgent. We need to know about it, for it exists, but none of the poems written there will be found in *Terra*. I guess that's another time-lapse, another book, another pocket. After *Hawkwood* came the more contemporary *London Poems* and others that were my snatchings at time and place already past among events already hurried into history: the South Atlantic war, the Libyan Embassy siege, sundry terrorist bloodbaths, various women bravely confronting missiles, the Miners' Strike, umpteen wobbles in the international jelly, and, meanwhile, contemporary life in a contemporary western city. Newsreel and footage, and voices off. In the end I made a joke, about the telegrams I never sent, and hope the joke is dark enough. In any case, I'm grateful someone on the PBS saw it, and herewith thankyou.

Getting a Result: *Wormwood* (1987)

The book is named for HM Prison Wormwood Scrubs, where I was writer in residence during the period of its writing. In the two years I was there I became quite obsessed with prison, with prison's inhabitants, with the place prison occupies in the public's consciousness. For two years I went in and (thankfully) out again, crossing the border of the gate between the strange closed world of maximum security and, whenever I came out, what had become the more estranged world of the outside.

In all its rigorous and Victorian dreariness, the Scrubs lies at the heart of this book. Not all the poems in the book sprang directly from the Scrubs, though everything in it falls within the timescale, and is in some baleful way influenced by the prison and the men I worked with. Many of them figure here, along with words they used. Showing the resulting poems to them – with considerable trepidation – I was gratified to find that they identified themselves and their predicament therein. Their criticisms at times led me to make changes; it was a rare opportunity to sample feedback, and to make use of it. More often, as poets, we work alone, and when (if ever) the responses come back it's too late to change what's in print, and we've moved on. Here I enjoyed a rare immediacy, and – as they say in prison of any positive response – *I got a result.*

Bodies

Some whose eyes I don't meet,
hands I don't shake, one that cut
NF in a man's back and left him
choke on his testicles, the knife
still in him and ran with the video.

Some with no story to bring sleep
or get supper and no tale
travellers repeat. He can say
I was responsible, can't say
I killed her, shot her, took an axe
and cut her to pieces, sawed her up
with the breadknife we'd used
so many years cutting our bread.

He asks himself over and over
what name her teeth had bit back
in her long coming, her *tsunami*
she called it in the pluperfect.
How when he'd phoned she was
never at home so where was she?

*

Charged with looking at the building.
In evidence a white male in a dark Allegro.
Some with a bottle, some with a needle.

Late afternoon the white meat waggons
roll in the day's catch, remanded
without bail, some misfit, some vicious,
the accused to be numbered.

*

Chalkie White, Metal Mickey, Spider Webb,
so where be they now? Last seen
with Murphy of Shepherd's Bush Boots,
helping Sgt E.C.T. Brainfuck from Paddington Green.
Last heard of on the block, on the book,
on the muffin run to Brixton.

Just helping Bill with his enquiries.

This one's Bungalow: no top storey.
This one's Muzz. And this one
singing in the canteen clatter at noon
I'm nobody's child, I'm nobody's child.
And no wonder another voice calls
down the wing as the neon hush falls
across paperwork and it's two hours
to unlock in the empire of the chinagraph.

Time to reflect:
                he hit her with a bottle,
a sewing machine, a chair, a tennis racket.
Offered her the easy way with aspirin.
Hit her twice when once was twice enough.

At the centre of the labyrinth: a rose.
At the centre of the rose's labyrinth: a worm.

The heart, the border (1990)

My last book of poems, *Wormwood*, together with the prose book, *Inside Time*, were attempts to work through my system the obsession with prison that developed during my time working at HMP Wormwood Scrubs from 1985 to 1987. Back then it seemed, no other subject so forcefully presented itself to me as the fact of imprisonment and its effects both on the convicted and their guardians; for most of them there is really only one theme, so that in the end it is the mind we imprison. Like all habitués of prison I too could talk of nothing else, or else of nothing at all. If prison darkened my life I was not unhappy about it; it was only that I wanted to write of something else from time to time. I was becoming restricted in my preoccupation, a one subject writer, and after the publication of *Wormwood* I resolved either to broaden my range or give up writing for a time.

I needed to escape from the thought of prison as much as from the definitions I had created for myself from writing about it; as Mrozek has it in his Nobel Prize speech, I needed to 'escape forward'. If that meant not writing, where writing meant repeating, so be it. There were occasions when, a new poem first presenting itself in a scatter of images, words, phrases, a vague disconnected music becoming clearer with listening, I would find it slyly turning into yet another poem about prison. Most of those poems I deliberately suppressed; those I let through into this book were either summations or valedications, final farewells to figures in the landscape.

So I decided to get away from it all and travelled, sometimes in Eastern Europe, where the borders were beginning to open. And as I crossed them I began to think about borders, the frontiers of political states, the magic line where the writ of one régime runs out and another begins, where definitions of right and wrong can interchange. And I began to think about the borders and limits of the self, of sanity and health and relationship, between psychological states, between waking and sleeping, dreaming and reason, the past and the future whose moving frontier is the present. And death, whose miserable border is crossed only once. With a heart attack I had in 1988 I thought I came near it, and thereafter it seems I endured a long silence, and slow beginnings. I had, at any rate, interrupted my obsession with confinement.

Later that same year, staring at the Berlin Wall behind which 17 million people were confined, I realised I had found myself a new subject, the image on the cover of the book, the heart on the border. I stayed with it, going back again and again through the Wall and then (there was no connection) the Wall opened, and the millions poured out from their prison. The result, written in tandem with *The heart, the border* and published at the same time (by Hamish Hamilton), is another prose book: *Berlin: Coming in from the Cold*.

Katja's message:

'This sentence has no meaning,
but what are you going to do about the crocodiles?'

In Berlin, attempting sleep, this sentence
without meaning keeping me awake;
one by one the hours climb the clock,
labour as slowly down the other side.

The silence at the border is absolute,
full of watching darkness, wire and neon,
the dark trees either side without wind
or weather or the baying of dogs.

It goes on and on, the silence, a lake
without a name where legends surface:
a bead of air, a log of wood, a skin,
an eye blinked open in the dark.

It is the crocodile, easing down
into another sleepless night
along the border, here beside the wall,
where still this sentence has no meaning.

Masks and Mirrors:
Tender to the Queen of Spain (1993)

It was a spring afternoon in Weymouth, and I was wandering about the stony harbour amongst fishing boats and yachts and tarted up trawlers, and there, upside down on trestles, being scraped and readied for painting by two workmen, was a large row boat. Upside down, I had to tip my head to read its name: it was the tender to a larger boat, it was the Tender to *The Queen of Spain*, a ship not around that day.

With one word, how many worlds we may visit. Ah, to be tender to the Queen of Spain: tender as in soft, delicate, fragile, loving. I thought of Columbus, returning home under storm, sleepless, fearful, writing frantic letters to Isabella, Queen of Aragon and Castile. And then: tender as in money or service; tender as one who works an engine or cares for a garden or works a bar; tender as a ship that leans under sail; tender as a crank, that gets something going.

And so the title, stumbled on, got me going, kicked me off. Serendipity has always been my way of working, more so as the years go by, as I learn to let go more. To be open to the incidental and the accidental, to suggestion and association, constitutes for me most of the business of being a poet.

Mostly it is a passive condition, this being open, receptive, though an active intention underlies it all, if only a busyness with something else, and when the moment arrives it must be seized, remembered. So wherever I go I carry a notebook and a pen, and the rest is a process of recording, and then – later, sometimes much later – working on this raw material of notes provoked by accidental recognitions and hidden connections to turn it into something finished: the poem. It can begin anywhere. It can begin with a line overheard in the street. *Read The World* I recall seeing once, a sticker on the side of a van. Well, I know *The World* is a newspaper, and that this injunction was merely a commercial message, a slogan or a jingle, but I read it as a larger command, a pressing message: read the world.

And so I read the world, which as ever is at once a place of terror and of beauty, a comedy full of tragedy and cruelty, a narrowing passage with only one exit at its end. I read its masks and its messages, and shape them into what makes sense to me, though I'll never know how much sense my poems make to anyone else. The century gets darker, and as we learn more it seems we understand less.

In and out of these poems are faces and voices: faces of the masks I make for myself out of chicken wire and papier mâché, newsprint colouring and bits of beads, earrings, tassles, feathers, junk I pick up in the street: Brother Scratchwood, Jack the old soldier, La Rosa – who is also Spanish queen – and the many characters of 'Three in a play'. Most of the masks I make form into groups of three: the three cruel mercenaries who are variously Stick, Twist, Trump, and also Thump, Boot and Headbutt, and also the knight, death and the devil; and all these are only three actors in a play who are *Umbilicus, the young naval attaché, Scrotum, the wrinkled old retainer, Sputum, a Flemish outcast.*

And all the other masks we all wear in the world: the masks we present to our mirrors.

And finally, as metaphor, *Tender to the Queen of Spain* is what it began as: a boat, ferrying stores and passengers between ship and shore. May God bless her, and all who sail in her.

Swag-bag of a word thief:
Wild Root (1998)

Wild root – a contradiction, a paradox, a species of tumbleweed, the name of a place far to the west, or maybe a woman's secret name for her lover that's no secret any more. Some years ago I invented a press whose only publication was the first version of my long poem *Fox Running* and called it Rolling Moss. Same idea. An image of the tension between the desire to stay home with the one I love and grow tomatoes in my own neck of the neighbourhood, and the longing 'to goon' as Chaucer remarks – 'on pilgrimages', usually in the spring – surely an ancient seasonal urge. 'Whan that Aprill with his shoores soote...' 'The winds of March that made my heart a dancer.'

For I love travelling, and I enjoy exploring strange cities, other people's countries, places where I haven't a clue in the language, and figuring it out. Or not, as the case may be. I dread departures: 'no man above mould...that before seafaring does not fear a little / whither the Lord will lead him in the end'. I love arrivals, and then moving on, but most I love coming home again with objects found along the way, tales to tell, characters to describe, new jokes, pages of my notebook covered in scribblings. Somehow I keep travelling further and further east, where lately I've been dumbstruck by the Carpathians and the Caucasus, wondering to which peak Prometheus was chained. In Tbilisi I heard a cock crowing, his call a distinct *Cau-ca-si-an* that he cried repeatedly to announce his identity. No self-doubt there. And in the same dark marvellous mad city I talked with a woman called Medea who was from western Georgia – Greek Colchis – and whose hair was a silver rather than a golden fleece, and no, she had never murdered her children.

Neruda: 'I take great vacations outside of time.' And Dr Johnson, more soberly: 'The use of travel is to regulate imagination with reality.' I don't know that travel broadens the mind, but it surely whips things up in there. The fact is if I don't take long journeys and meet different strangers, I grow blunt and rusty like a knife left out in the rain. I think of the world as a great marketplace where I go hunter–gathering for images and words and ideas.

'Two hearts for fifty pence,' a woman calls on my local market. She's selling lettuces. And a white van goes by bearing the slogan *'Read the World'*. That's what I'm doing, that's what I do. I'm an earwigger and an observer. I frequent railway stations and markets and the back of magistrates' courts, and nip in and out of guided tours, and anything that appeals to me in the way of words I'll snatch into my notebook, perhaps to appear later as the occasion of a poem or just a voice flitting through: 'Tarbert, this godforsaken hole: I've seen better on a card of buttons: waggontruss, windbrace; I was one chopstick short of a pot noodle.' I'm a word thief, and don't care what the sources are. For me there's no pecking order as to where the words come from: books, overheard in the pub or on a bus, glimpsed from the corner of an eye in a newspaper someone else is reading, machine language, graffiti: they're all interesting. Speaking of graffiti, here's one from the men's room of a bar in Cambridge, Mass.: 'The only time I ever refused a drink I misunderstood the question.'

And when I'm home there's still the tomatoes, and from time to time I make masks out of chicken wire and papier maché. It distracts me, keeps my hands busy so my mind is free to wander, and sometimes when a face begins to form from the mess of paper and paste, questions swim up as to who this character is, and sometimes there's someone with a name and a history. Sometimes it may be just a line, or the start of something. And sometimes the whole poem. My methods are serendipity. I've been called a bricoleur, someone forever reassembling the broken bits of the world into new shapes. I thought the word, in Lévi-Strauss's term, meant beachcomber, but when I looked it up I found it defined as a do–it–yourselfer. I really don't mind; I'm easy with both definitions. Serendipity. I like lists. Fact is I'm a collector of junk, 'scavenger of skips' always on the look-out for surprises, hidden links, coincidences, images and phrases to be recycled. I collect postage stamps, signs, tickets, maps, books, sardine tins, shells, stones, feathers, buttons, leaves, bits of wood river-scrubbed into the faces of animals and birds, a compartmented box for a collection of toy legs found in the street, a board for the tacked-up gleanings of the beach at Guincho in Portugal, furthest point west of Europe, so they say. And a rare treasure, found abandoned in a hotel drawer, that felt addressed to me: *Catalogue d'objets introuvables*, by Jaques Carelamns, published by France Loisirs, Paris, 1969, a marvellous collection of drawings of impossible and therefore undiscoverable objects.

And borders, in all their manifestations, fascinate me, those tense edgy places of walls and fences and boundaries – borders political and geographic and psychological, transitions between one condition and the next: past and future, sanity and nonsense, life and death. Passing through them is to enter a place where the rules have changed, and are unknown, and this focuses my attention, so that I think in travelling I'm honing the edges of my hearing, sharpening the blades of words. Words, words, words. And another collection, of visas and passport stamps. 'I am the Emperor, and I want noodles.'

Why I write

Why I write: to try to make sense of this babbling lunacy. I think to myself: if the extra-terrestrials ever make it here, wherever they land that will be who they talk to, and they'll take them for the norm of our species. Think about it: they land in Afghanistan where they meet the Taliban, who treat them as infidels and won't let them use paper bags in case they are made from recycled paper on which, once, were written the words of the Prophet. Or say Montreal, where they'd be in trouble with the Language Police if the signs on their vehicles weren't written in French. It all depends on who you ask. As to our own version of civilised behaviour, it ain't necessarily so that any of it is *normal*. We just think it is, and go on selling landmines to the warring states, and giving more and more to the rich.

So it's a constant shoring up in a world governed by the laws of entropy and a universe that, according to recent measurements of its density, thins out forever into an endless diaspora of dead stars getting further and further away from each other, and no one to remark on it. For now there is writing, what we call literature, which as John Barthes has said is a one-way conversation in time, a river of voices thinking aloud that can be listened to over millennia: *I can still hear Homer. I can still hear John Milton, and William Blake.* And maybe if I stick at it I can join the conversation.

But I don't think about it much, and aren't much interested in the critical and theoretical. My own behaviour makes sense to me, but to anyone else they would note that in the last couple of months I have (1) demolished a wall in my house and made a hell of a mess, so much so my nearest and dearest really thought I had flipped this time, and (2) buggered off to the Outer Hebrides for a week on a sudden whim to get as far north as I could, and (3) set fire to my telephone. What kind of tale might be made of these three for starters? What kind of sense?

And that's all folks.

[1997]

Ken Smith inhabiting Fox's urban terrain: London, 1982.

'Best, Ken': Letters and an Interview

THE HOLE IN THE TOOTH

It was in the somewhat costive environment of a so-called "alternative" bookshop in York, around 1981-82, that I first encountered Ken Smith's poetry. Something akin to a manila envelope was sticking out from a bottom shelf, like an electricity bill wedged in a letterbox. I bent down and slid out a pamphlet entitled *Fox Running*. It was about the size of an average place-mat and the colour of a digestive biscuit. I remember flipping through the pages and coming across the set of quatrains that start, 'Beginning again and again / Beginning from what's broken.' The force with which these lines came off the page was staggering. I had never read anything like them. Being a good East Riding lad, i.e. – a tad frugal, I still hesitated to buy the poem though, but then relented: £1.50.

I surely wasn't the only 20 nothingmuch nosing around at that time for a poetry which caught something of the charged air of living in a city – the mood and atmosphere, the energy and the volatility – its sights and sounds every bit as visceral as those of the countryside. At the universities and colleges Philip Larkin was still being presented as the urban poet, yet his observations seemed to take place at such a remove. The synecdochic detailing was masterful, the muted lyricism beguiling, but the wistful, melancholic tone seemed to screen out as much as it showed. For many, city life was a much more abrasive affair.

And that's what *Fox Running* (1980) portrays. Fleeing to inner London from a 'broken' marriage, without employment or funds, the central figure is exposed to the impact of the social and political forces of the city in a particularly acute manner. The intensity of the narrative voice is immediately striking. The account is relayed with great urgency and compression, yet fiercely controlled and syncopated. There is a real sense of the drama of an encounter, of Fox's noir-lit attempt to cognitively map his estranging surroundings. The indignities and distress of his personal life are exacerbated by the indifference and waste he finds 'way down Thatcherland' (*Poet Reclining*, 163), and overlapping impressions are absorbed at an angle determined by hurt. Without emotional shelter or the protection of a secure role in society, Fox runs to sustain a scavenged existence and keep at bay the reproaches of his own inner monologue. He

runs to outrun defeat. Hence the urgency of the quatrains, registered
in the abrupt rhythms and curt ellipsis:

> Holed up with Baudelaire and Lorca.
> On Sundays picking up exotic fruit
> along the market side, selling
> half a dozen ties he's nicked.
>
> Back of Dingwalls where the lads
> were selling junk. His mad and
> staring eyes. His mouth
> repeating how she was his sparrow.
>
> How she was his woman, faithless
> as the wind turns anywhere, he'd been
> better bedded with the wind
> or wedded to the water.
>
> Winter and summer all he loved
> lied to him when he'd not
> hurt anyone would he. Such
> were the gaps in his schedule.
>
> Such were his night thoughts.
> Other nights he'd off himself,
> fall into the rail, take his last
> white skittering glimpse of England
>
> down Beachy Head cliffs. Stain
> the rocks. Feed the ravens.
> Such was his nightly scenario,
> his single movie of himself.
>
> (*Poet Reclining*, 135)

When I interviewed Ken Smith in 1997 I characterised the rhythm
of lines like these from *Fox Running*, and others of a similar nature
from elsewhere in his work – lines which it seems to me show him
working at his most intense pitch – as possessing 'a driving vehe-
ment plainchant' quality, whereby phrases are 'jammed together,
shorn of elaboration and connectives, by a narrative urgency'.[1] In
his timely book, *Contemporary British poetry and the city*, Peter
Barry quotes this observation, only to turn it against the poem:
'The problem is, perhaps, that the very driving, vehement plain-
song which the animal persona seems to validate drives too fast
and fluently when the need is for some expression of hesitation,
confusion, and uncertainty.'[2] But what is so compelling about the
lines I've quoted is precisely the sudden switching between images,
thoughts and states of mind, reflecting as it does the twists and
turns of a consciousness caught in the net of its own pain, confu-
sion and uncertainty. In rapid succession, yes, though not without

subtle changes in pace, longing gives way to anger, self pity, then vengeful fantasy. When read aloud the speech cadences demand modulations in the tempo in order to fetch out particular feelings or attitudes. Note for example how the momentum of 'when he'd not / hurt anyone would he' brakes in order to dramatise the suspect indignation. As a description of the verse, 'fast and fluid' is simply inadequate. When read as a whole, the narrative trajectory is enacted by the poem's rhythmic score. It runs, then draws breath, runs again, until gradually the clearings of vision become more pronounced.

A crucial part of the appeal of *Fox Running* is the frank, unflinching depiction of the hero's own failings. The degree of emotional directness is unusual for a male English poet, but there is no sense of the self-inflation that can mar the work of "confessional" poets such as Sylvia Plath. The essentially quotidian language generates a tremendous heat, but it is almost ruthlessly contained by the terse phrasing and syntax. This is one source of the terrific tension in the following lines, where the desperation is made partially bearable by the mordant wit at Fox's own expense and the appalled, seaside-postcard humour:

> Happens. Crash. The fall from grace
> blind drunk into the orchestra,
> the bit where she sits peeling daisies
> saying she loves him loves him not.
>
> Sleepless. Nights the twenty years
> of loving her are all one string
> of beads on mother misery's rosary,
> and how she knew to put the boot in.
>
> And put the boot in. Lists his one last
> broken wedding dish, his one last cry
> in any corner, his one last cigarette,
> under the glittering dancehall ball
>
> their one last tango, one last fuck
> anywhere under the stars and how
> when his mouth said yes to her
> there was his penis saying *no no no.*
>
> (*Poet Reclining*, 136)

Barry yokes his criticism of a perceived undifferentiated pacing in the poem to the claim that its idiom is too Hughesian – that in fact it reads as if were 'written by Ted Hughes'.[3] Again this represents a serious mishearing of the poem. It simplifies a poet's voice, the essential fingerprint of his or her music, to a matter of diction alone. Though the two poets come from similar backgrounds and share a northern working-class vernacular as a first language, in one key aspect their basic approaches are very different. Not uncommonly, both drew attention to the strategies they favoured through praising particular qualities in the work of others. With regard to Hughes, one of the most telling instances of this occurred when he commented not upon a poem but simply another writer's manner of speaking when telling an anecdote. In an introduction written for a LAMDA anthology, Hughes refers to an interview with Walter de la Mare and how he was captivated by 'the slow musing phrases of his old but wonderfully alert and living voice, the surprised and surprising cadences of it'.[4] He characterised the effect as a 'delicate, searching, naked music'. And when writing at his most penetrating, isn't this precisely the note, the rhythmic pitch of attention, that he himself was seeking? For example, as in these gently probing lines from 'The Last of the 1st/5th Lancashire Fusiliers', where the right-branching syntax and eased-open cadence allow metaphor to slowly expose and develop an image of his father:

> Now he had become a long-billed, spider-kneed bird
> Bow-backed, finding his footing, over the frosty cobbles
> A wader, picking curiosities from the shallows.[5]

This is fine writing, but Smith was after something other than the lingering gaze dwelling on a single object. And pacing was critical. In a review of Sean O'Brien's *Cousin Coat: Selected Poems* he singled out his admiration for 'the speed…the efficiency with which the man gets where he's going, the prevalence of sharp short images that are kinetic, fast moving film as distinct from a succession of slides, that carry so much narrative freight'.[6] His analogy harks back to an assessment of his work first made by Roger Garfitt when reviewing *The Poet Reclining* in 1983: 'Poetry ceases to be what it is so often in England, an art of framed observations: it becomes the spelling out of a selfhood.'[7] This comment clearly became something of a touchstone for Smith. He referred to it approvingly in a number of interviews. No doubt he linked it with the phenomenon associated with the photographer Eadweard Muybridge, namely the persistence of vision, whereby a series of still pictures run at a particular speed give the appearance of continuous motion. 'The Persistence of Vision' was once the overarching working title of *Fox Running*,[8] and in the poem the concept seems to have acted as a structural metaphor for evading personal and cultural paralysis through seeking out continuities amidst disruption, and more immediately as a stylistic prompt, validating the swift juxtaposition of 'sharp short images' as a way of countering the grim static 'frame' of Fox's situation. In this context, rhythm becomes an existential matter. This was the point made by Tony Harrison in an interview with Richard Hoggart, when he commented on his own need for a 'strong rhythm' to act as 'a life support system', allowing him to 'go closer to the fire, deeper into the darkness', and yet still 'have this rhythm to carry [him] to the other side'.[9] 'Rhythm gives us the very psychic energy of the speaker' argued Roethke,[10] and in the firm, percussive momentum of the following quatrains, there is amongst other things a commitment to take on board all that has happened and come through:

> No way a fox goes out, no way
> a man who was fox, kept ignorant
> of what killed him, icy in the morgue,
> ashes in the crematorium, words
>
> entered in the black form filed away
> beside the red his birth was
> and between some forty years
> his blood pumped out of him
>
> the skylines that he crossed,
> his memory of ferns and rivers,
> distance, open country, city,
> women that he loved, songs he sang.
>
> Better die quick, if fox
> at the heels of the hounds, if man
> at the razor of some loonie. Better live
> and if living running better run.
>
> And keep running. Marylebone,
> Lisson Grove, Edgware Road to Kew
> to Wimbledon. Scattered sparks
> and windblown newsprint, coming out
>
> surprised again beside the river,
> images the city has, home
> the subway's groan and slide of pipes
> and checking out of maps, his skull
>
> encountering the city, his body
> moving with a certain grace,
> moving with particular intelligence
> across the city's interstices.
>
> And surviving through the rooms
> his flesh joins other flesh
> and makes some heat. Among
> the endless conversations, starts, stops,
>
> unfinished lives' biographies,
> feints, gestures, cries, his life's
> plain furniture, a borrowed room
> in Camden to begin again from nothing.

Thoughts of a man around 40.
Notes. Maps. Things missing.
People that he loved his life ran with
all gone now, gone forever.

(*Poet Reclining*, 137-38)

It is a ferocious piece of writing. Just in the final few lines we witness the remorseless starkness of the apprehension ('his flesh joins other flesh / and makes some heat'), the point-blank appraisal ('feints, gestures, cries, his life's / plain furniture, a borrowed room / in Camden to begin again from nothing'), the aching wryness ('Thoughts of a man around 40'), before the concluding stoic assessment ('all gone now, gone forever'). And everything is bound together by the strong heartbeat note of his own distinctive accentual voice.

When I asked Smith in the 1997 interview about the character-istic rhythmical impetus of his verse, he referred to it as a product of 'an emphatic list-making activity'.[11] He went on: 'Sometimes I think I'm a list-making animal. I try to list the essentials in any particular circumstance, in any particular situation.' Dubbed 'the heaping figure' by George Puttenham in his *The Arte of English Poesie*, the result of this list-making process is more generally known as congeries. More straightforwardly still, Smith viewed it as a matter of taking out the 'tightness...the stripping out of the extra-neous words, prepositions, punctuation'.[12] In his hands, this imparted a compaction and intensity reminiscent of Old English poetry – his great, enduring literary love. His favouring of lexical as opposed to function words also heightened the concreteness and physicality of his diction, giving body and momentum to his poetry.

There are of course dangers to adopting this approach. It can all become far too 'rum-ram-ruff' for some. It is the ghost of alliterative metre that haunts Smith's 'free verse', and as such his works stands at something of a tangent to the belief expressed by Ruth Padel that iambic pentameter is 'the magically flexible line which has dominated English aural imagination since the sixteenth century'.[13] It becomes a question of touch, tact – ear. And as Smith was developing his paratactic style in America during the early 70s, opinions differed among some of his poet-friends as to its effective-ness. When sent copies of the prose poems first collected in the pamphlet, *Frontwards in a backwards movie* (1975),[14] Jeffrey Wain-wright warned him of a tendency towards creating a 'perfunctory list', of becoming 'monotonous' and 'too muscular'.[15] Responding to the same volume, however, Ted Hughes praised Smith for putting together 'a beautiful sequence of pieces. Very hard and real...very bleak unique note. And mostly so different from each

101

other. Each one works like an opening into something different, and new.'[16]

Perhaps it is fair to say that Smith's poetry encompasses the qualities that both Wainwright and Hughes name. There is in his work a tension between that which is insistently compelling and that which is simply overplayed. At its least effective, there is less a sense of apprehension being contained than attenuated. Stanzas dwindle into collection points of inert noun phrases. But when energy and insight come together, the verse functions in a manner similar to that which Daniel Donoghue identifies as being typical of the appositive constructions in Old English poetry: 'Sometimes the effect is simply cumulative; at other times the repetition allows shifting perspectives to examine the same idea.'[17] Naturally it is difficult to quote briefly to illustrate cumulative effects, but the following small excerpt from 'The Shadow of God', *Wild Root* (1998), depicting the carnage resulting from sultan Suleyman's onslaught through Hungarian marshlands in 1526, effectively demonstrates Smith's mastery of the swift 'efficiency' he admired in O'Brien's poetry:

> No prisoners,
> the wails of the wounded, the dying, becks
> brimmed with blood, and the young King
> thrown from his horse, drowned in his breastplate.
>
> (*Shed*, 270)

What we can see here is how the Old English metrical template allows for the grammatical loosening that Smith sought while facilitating narrative compression. The account does not dawdle or drift. Unlike in most Old English poetry, however, the alliteration spans the run-on line, underscoring how running on is Smith's way. As for the telling juxtaposition of different viewpoints, only a few lines later we read:

> And thereafter, pronounces the historian,
> his quill's tip brushing his cheek, his point
> squeaking over the page, the lamp's glint
> on his inkhorn: *the long Turkish night,*
> *the tomb of the nation,* dug in the rain.
>
> (*Shed*, 271)

The careful parallelism and cinematic detailing intensify the evaluative crux registered in the last line, its medial caesura effectively counterpointing two perspectives: the historian's laboured conceit is pitched against – and exposed by – the narrator's pithy eloquence.

Though as prone as any other stylistic trait to becoming a mannerism, this kind of abrupt phrasing is at heart something quite different from literary affectation. For Smith it seems to have been integral to his sense of himself as a writer. In the above extract, the narrator is resisting not just the rhetorical flourish, but also the complacency of the accompanying worldview. Resistance is the key word. A number of commentators have remarked upon the almost familial abrasiveness of a range of contemporary writers associated with the north of England, and Linden Peach has described this as a cultural predilection, 'part of the attempt to resist larger hegemonic forces...part of the attempt to find a language that will enable them to express their own, resistant sense of identity'.[18] This is well expressed, and Smith's susceptibility to this stance would have been only strengthened by his time at Leeds University during the early 60s, the acquaintances and friendships he made there, including crucially with Jon Silkin and Geoffrey Hill, and his joint-editing of *Stand* magazine from 1963 to 1969. Having said that, he seems to have arrived there already temperamentally predisposed towards an abrasive, questioning posture. As it did throughout his writing career, this gave him the angle, the slant, he required to tell his truths. For instance, consider how he was able to deflect off the trenchant note struck by a clause in Sidney Keyes' 'William Wordsworth', and three lines from a Mao Tse-tung poem, to produce 'Family group' and 'The pity' respectively, those great early poems written back to back within the space of one week in the summer of 1963 and collected in his first volume, *The Pity* (1967).[19]

The following lines from 'The pity' show the power of Smith's writing was there from the start:

> But the cockroach and the grinning toad
> drawn beautiful was China; the fly grown fat on flesh,
> glittering in heat. I was lashed and drained
> of the gentle passion. Patience was prised from me.
> I picked lice from my hair. You thought me gentle still.
> I ate filth, wore it, would have died in filth.
>
> (*Poet Reclining*, 17)

It is a riveting account, and marks Smith's first use of a mask voice. Mao's outrage at his humiliation is first caught by the force of the verbs and plosives, and then contained by the tight alliterative binding and half-line breaks. There is also a marvellous momentary change in key, slipping into *sotto voce* – 'You thought me gentle still' – as though the speaker suddenly looks to his side to address a feminine presence, the tone of the half declarative, half interrogative statement being simultaneously rueful, tender and pained. Smith's ability to empathise with Mao's plight might well have been kindled by witnessing his father's frustration and growing anger when the move from being a tenant farmer to running a grocer's shop in Hull failed to appease his gnawing dissatisfaction with his life. This is vividly portrayed in 'Family group' (see pages 69-70 of this volume). The weighted drag of the syntax in the last verse paragraph is particularly effective in evoking a feeling of sub-jugation, while the imagery conveys nothing so much as live en-tombment. It is as though his father too is imprisoned – in this instance, between the walls of his shop. Though Smith's writing of the *Wormwood* poems was 30 years off, in a sense his exploration of a fettered '8 by 12' mentality had begun. It is a frightening pic-ture of holed-up masculinity, baited by its own exasperation.

If the reference to, and reversal of, a line from Wordworth's 'Old Man Travelling' ('A man who does not move with pain, but moves / With thought') might suggest Smith was adopting a simplistic Romantic paradigm, country *v.* city, this is far from the case.[20] The opposition is much more carefully weighed, the rigour of the family's life on farms depicted in full earlier in the poem; and in another piece from the same volume the estrangement his father experienced when working the land surfaces more strongly – in part, despite Smith's efforts. The drafts of the poem 'Country: Keld to Reeth' show how divided he was on the matter. Through a number of initial versions, a representation of dyadic unity, nature and man, is broached only to be instantly withdrawn:

> My father surely
> I glimpsed you between the faces of horses,
> gentle as the beasts standing to be milked.
>
> Your head did not rest on their bellies.
> You did not pause on the hill. This was not
> your country also.

In the poem published in *The Pity*, this conflict is reduced to, 'Returning, he did not pause on the hill / between the still faces of horses' (*Poet Reclining*, 15), though in the penultimate stanza he seems to offset the finality of this judgement by insisting –

> Neither nation nor map, I keep
> only this mind's country:
> farms and sheep crouched in together,
> an eternal rooting of grass,
> communion of roots and the gripped soil,
> weather,
> cattle,
> men.
>
> (*The Pity*, 20)

When he subsequently included this poem in *The Poet Reclining*

(1982), these lines were cut. This then leaves the starkness of the final stanza unqualified:

> The hills lie on anvils of stone,
> sheepcut, shaped by all weathers.
> Great stones squat on the ridges
> as if the ice might come back for them.
> A few harebells lift to the wind.
> There is a ragged field, patches of bramble.
>
> (*Poet Reclining*, 15)

Again Smith revisits Wordsworth, this time 'Resolution and Independence', his use of 'squat' as opposed to 'couched' to describe the stones resting on the hills managing to telescope into a single word the inference of the earlier poet's ambivalent 'sea-beast' imagery.[21] That is, the emptiness of the scene is edged with menace: it somehow manages to be both perfectly commonplace and slightly alarming at one and the same time. The significance of this is that, for Smith, this was the landscape of his childhood, a terrain pervaded by the movements of his temperamental father. It was also, as the finally deleted stanza indicated, his 'mind's country'.

These three poems are probably the most accomplished of his early work. Elsewhere the vitality of the laconic phrasing is often undermined by an earnest, monologic tone. He had yet to come free of his influences, and even a piece such as 'The Wood', the final poem collected in *The Pity*, and up to that point his most ambitious in narrative scope, still feels constricted by the austerity of the Johannes Bobrowski-inspired short lines and the Silkin-like mode of address: 'Being alive – / is not simple... Feeling love, pity, is it nothing / I ask / that the beasts do not do so' (*The Pity*, 60). During the middle 60s Smith seems to have lost his way slightly. Though initially instructive, his close alliance with Silkin appears to have become constraining. Surprisingly, given that 'The pity' and 'Family group' are among the finest poems written by any English writer during this period and show Smith beginning to stake out his own territory, he allowed himself to become locked into the binarism of the grass and stone – pity and apathy – schema which Silkin was exploring during these years. Aware that this was happening, for a time there was a feeling around for focus, for where to go next.

This is why the time he spent in America from 1969 to 1973 was so important to him. Though initially daunting, it completed the break begun in 1965 when he moved from Leeds to Exeter. Smith was now on his own and in an alien environment, operating without the support of the *Stand*, Leeds or even English literary scene; but he also felt himself to be free of the accompanying injunctions, and not for the last time in his writing career he found these conditions and the space that opened up before him as exciting as it was intimidating. Put simply, part of what he was looking to break free from was the manner in which up to that point he had written poems. As I've just indicated, my own estimation of 'The pity' and 'Family group' is extremely high, but I doubt he shared it. They never, for instance, featured in any of the readings I attended, though he would occasionally read something dating back to the early 1970s. The construction of these poems represented a way of working, a way of thinking, he wanted to get away from. Even in the lines from 'The pity' quoted above, the opening statement – 'But the cockroach and the grinning toad / drawn beautiful was China' – has a didactic, essay-like quality which he increasingly found unappealing. It smacks of something too heavily plotted and planned. As he explained it to me:

> The early poems came about through being screwed up, working at it, typing hard, generally making a lot of fuss about a poem. I mean I think that even poems like 'The pity' and 'Family group' are still too hammered, they're still too worked, they're still too punched...As a working method it's screwing you up.[22]

One of his first 'America' poems was 'Inventory / Itinerary'. I'll quote this interesting piece in full; although collected in *Work, distances/ poems* (1972), it did not make the selection for *The Poet Reclining*:

> Illinois, Iowa
> Dead grass & maize stalks
> Miles, miles, 4 1/2 thousand
> Timeshift 7 hours
> 2 continents, 1 ocean
> Travelling, 4 days
> 1 good time, much being quiet
> 200 cigarettes, 1 bottle brandy
> 1 arrival in Iowa City
> March 25th 1969, 6.00pm
> $3.38 in my pocket
> 1 cab-ride into the clapboard wilderness
> 1 return on foot carrying 2 bags
> 9 phone calls, two wrong numbers, 1 reply
> Waiting, waiting
> Hunger, loneliness, weariness, silence
> 1 poem written quickly holding things down
> The durations of wind, cold, grainfields
> Endless helpfulness, cheerfulness, on the nail
> The bland faces, America, America
> And silence. And night
> And wind blowing, right through the heart
>
> (*Work, distances/ poems*, 25)

Though it is clearly a fairly basic prototype of the style Smith was to evolve, there is nevertheless an engaging listing of the essentials here. It could be usefully viewed as a stripping down of his usual method of proceeding in order to sharpen his ability to respond to immediate experience. What he found so exhilarating about the American literary scene was that just this kind of basic re-evaluation of approach was much more widely on the agenda. It was less that he followed the practice of any of the individuals he was reading at the time – people like Robert Bly, James Wright and W.S. Merwin – and more that he was able to draw on the general air of reappraisal in which they were all in involved. Reflecting on this period and the relationship of his work with that of Bly, Wright and others, Merwin himself has commented:

> We didn't so much influence each other as feel the same things. It was perfectly clear that the things I had felt as a kind of straitjacket could be broken out of after all. The straitjacket really wasn't there. We didn't have to pay attention to it any more. [...] We were throwing out all of the apparatus of literary careers and everything, saying, 'Ah, that's not important; what's important is writing a different kind of poem.' [23]

For Bly, the free verse or open form they were employing was not a literary technique, but 'a step in growth…a way to encourage [us] to let up a little in repression, ease up the projection, and move out a bit from the lowest stage of consciousness'.[24] Smith, too, sought to 'ease up' on the leading protagonist of *The Pity*, to encourage the sometimes uptight first person narrator to break free of his own 'straightjacket'. In the context of what was said earlier, there was an opening of his stance during these years, an attempt to be more alert and flexible in terms of how he acted upon and developed the material that engaged him – from both within and without. Regarding the advance he felt he made while in America, he said: 'I think for me it was a matter of learning to recognise daydreams and sleeping dreams and to draw images from areas like that.'[25]

As was the case with 'The pity', the use of a mask voice was a critical factor, and with 'Dream journeys' for instance, first published in *Work, distances/ poems*, he rediscovered the authority of the earlier poem, while unfolding this storyteller's tale with a more supple muscularity and a less schematic inner structure. This gives rise to a central issue with regard to Smith's work. It is not that he promptly abandoned metrical constraints in America. For all the increased compositional freedom he allowed himself, there is still a strong sense of control. In 'Dream journeys', as in the related Native American persona poems, such as 'Crying woman', 'Song for the whites' and 'The Sioux cleared from Minnesota', a niggling anxiety as to co-opting the experience of others and a continuing attachment to a compact rhythmic measure, ensure that his lines rarely simply unfurl across the page. This was to remain the case throughout the succeeding years. Even when he's 'on a roll', as he termed it in the 1997 interview, and there's a sure sense of 'this voice coming through', supervisory direction is evident.[26] His lines seldom sprawl with Ginsbergian largesse. The 'roll' is staggered, sectioned, into phrasal – and then narrative – units. Even at his most relaxed, Smith's inclination for thinking in half lines, like the Anglo-Saxon *scops*, is never far from view. There is in his poetry a vitalising interplay between a desire for the free flowing and an instinct for the bitten-back. In 'Dream journeys', the prickly defer-ence evident in the extract from 'The Wood' has gone, to be replaced by a tempered expansiveness reminiscent of certain Latin American poets. Like the figure they describe, the lines move with 'an easy care', yet take us right to the core of Smith's concerns:

> At the last
> he walked between land and sea, a man
> centuries old stepping the waterline stones
> with an easy care, his eye never to one side
> but to the edge of water and haze, and stepping so
> a child came whom he seized and ate,
> throwing aside what was half-eaten
> as he came to the distance, without pause.

> (*Poet Reclining*, 30)

Tracking the border between land and water, the man might almost be a sudden personification of the malign force – the shadow side of Wordsworth's strange sea-beast – alluded to in 'Country: Keld to Reeth'. Certainly it is an unnerving invocation of a demonic masculinity. This is how Smith described the origin of the poem:

It was I recall a very powerful dream, in which the figure on the shore-line appears and behaves as described, and there's nothing to be done about it; the child is dead. I guess it was related to being a father of young children, and one's anxieties over what can happen, the inexpli-cable and irrational act of pure malice. Recently I was talking to an exile Serb writer (an old hack, in fact, an apparatchik, former Yugoslav ambassador to Ghana when the squashy stuff hit the fan); anyway, he was talking about this figure in their mythology, which as far as I can see has no correspondence in any of our mythologies, Celtic or Nordic or Latin or Greek: the Herostrat, the figure who fucks everything up, destroys everything, for no reason at all.[27]

'The Eli Poems' were also prompted by a disturbing dream, or rather series of dreams, though this time the masculine violence, the casually brutal treatment of a young woman by an older man, only pushed Smith to venture more deeply into himself and achieve a newly tender and sensuous realisation of the feminine:

> I married a crazy woman for her brown hair.
> At first I thought she was pregnant
> but her blood runs, the doctor shakes his head at me.
> I tell her your child is in the other country
> and will not come here because of your frenzy.
> She runs to the church crying she's evil,
> the priest holds out his god's battered arms
> and says *come child everyone's evil.*
> I cool her with my breath, I cool her with water.
>
> ('Eli's poem'; *Poet Reclining*, 60-61)

> In the room now I breathe
> for the smell of you, your thighs
> wet as horses' flanks in harvest,
> your heat's dumb flailing.
>
> Dust you breathed, memory
> of your throat-sound, your sweat
> ingrained in my flesh,
> a stained quilt, survive you.
>
> ('The rooming house'; *Poet Reclining*, 61-62)

A bewildered, grief-charged lyric voice is the visible thread running through this narrative sequence.

By the autumn of 1973 Smith was back in England and based once more in Exeter. No doubt the distances he had covered and the relative ease of access to the *Exeter Book*, encouraged a sense of affiliation with the wanderer figure of that text; but it is hardly unusual for writers to either go to America or to travel around more generally in order to secure work. What made Smith's identification with kinless wanderers, with outlawed/outsider figures, so pronounced? One way of answering is to consider the centrality to his work of 'Being the third song of Urias' (*Poet Reclining*, 172-73), a poem first published in 1980 and one with which he often began a reading. Once again we are taken back to his childhood and his 'mind's country'.

Deixis is a commonly employed term in stylistics and has been defined as referring to 'all those features of language which orientate or "anchor" our utterances in the context of space and of time relative to the speaker's viewpoint'.[28] I mention it here because what is most immediately unsettling about the opening lines of 'Being the third song of Urias' is the marked disruption of usual deictic expectations. Reading, 'Lives ago, years past generations / perhaps nowhere I dreamed it', we experience a sharp sense of temporal and spatial dislocation. The lack of punctuation, the compacting of locative expressions to the point where they start to cancel each other out, frustrates rather than confirms our sense of time and place. Moreover, when a concrete reference point is introduced, its outline is initially blurred by the accompanying modifier, 'the foggy ploughland', before then being temporarily erased through a combination of the prepositional phrase extension and line break, 'of wind / and hoofprints'. In short, the poem's location becomes a ghostly terrain of traces out of which looms an absent presence, isolated by the succeeding line break: 'my father / off in the mist topping beats'.

In retrospect, this ominous disembodied sighting calls to mind the spectral figures alluded to and then envisaged in 'Country: Keld to Reeth' and 'Dream journeys' respectively. The poem goes on to be a conjuring of Smith's first world, a domain of vivid sentient impressions – 'the white rime on weeds / among the wet hawthorn berries / at the field's edge darkened by frost' – repeatedly fractured by outbursts of male anger, his father's 'gregarious plainchant cursing / all that his masters deserved'. The clear inference is that the founding disorientation in Smith's life originated in the aftermath of his father's explosive rage. There was a shattering of concord between self and world, and relating to it thereafter became a matter of 'beginning from what's broken'.

Not unreasonably, his father's 'cursing' could be interpreted as a product of class anger, but other pieces by Smith suggest this was not the whole story. What intensified the impact of these fits of temper still further was the eerie silence that followed. Although his father's rage was often 'gregariously' expressed, what lay behind it, beyond the immediate trigger of workplace disgruntlement, was never voiced. His father would not talk of his past. This lack of disclosure alone appears to have haunted Smith, necessitating his constant mental return to a spectral site, doubly 'darkened' by his father's heavily guarded unhappiness:

> I began trailing out there in voices,
> friends, women, my children,
> my father's tetherless anger, some
> like him who are dead who are
> part of the rain now.

What this final stanza forcefully conveys is a sense of the poet's ghostly inheritance, revealing a fissured and pluralised subjectivity, traversed by the calls of others, and both augmented and burdened as a result. In such a fog-bound arena, familial ordeal merges almost imperceptibly with collective trauma – as though one cry in the dark attracts others, until the presentiment of a caravan of voices reaching back into time, the displaced and the marginalised, the rejected and the scorned, the imprisoned and the dead, becomes a felt reality. In this scenario his father appears as something of a link-figure, the gatekeeper, fearsome, destructive, anguished, helpless.

Figuratively, these voices are represented as being as nebulous and pervasive as the weather. They determine the emotional climate of his mind. Viewed from this perspective, writing, the attempt to find some stable clearing of vision, seems less chosen than compelled, even though the act has been ironically subverted earlier in the poem:

> Before like a fool I began
> explaining the key in its lost locked box
> adding words to the words to the sum
> that never works out.

To search for the linguistic 'key' to the personal and historical up-heaval of even the recent past where so much has been abandoned, broken or simply hidden, means constantly coming across remnants and vestiges. Piecing together these verbal and visual fragments is deemed to be an ultimately forlorn attempt to clarify an under-standing that 'never works out'. In other words, Smith sees his task as that of a Blakeian 'fool', who nevertheless feels impelled to persist 'in his folly'. He keeps 'trailing out there'.

The poem is as much a mission statement as it is an *ars poetica*, suggesting why Smith felt so drawn to speaking for those who either could not or would not. What happened in his childhood was an unhealed wound to which he returned again and again. When I asked him in the 1997 interview whether he agreed with a notion expressed by Peter Redgrove,[29] that every poet had within them one central poem and that individual poems represented fragments of it, he replied:

> I'm sympathetic to it. It would be hard for me to see all my work as one poem, but there are some specific strands of meaning and theme, certain obsessive images and ideas, that run through the whole lot. In that sense it may be one life's work and maybe it is one long poem. I think we keep going back to the same hole in the tooth where you stick your tongue in and it hurts. Therefore my father keeps recurring, there-fore certain themes keep recurring – borders, perspectives, visions...I'm still trying to make sense of it. I may never succeed, but if I quit then I won't make any sense at all.[30]

It is hardly a comfortable proposition to hold, to envisage your psyche as a thoroughfare trafficked by the shards of lost voices, the hurt, abused, angry and grieving, all those wanting recompense. His use of the injured mouth analogy seems important, implying that as a poet he could not only register the pain but also seek to articulate it. He seems to have increasingly felt that this was the crucial advantage he had over the illiterate, uncommunicative father whom he loved – his craft as a word*smith*, a pun he himself used: that by asyndetically splicing fragments together across a medial caesura there was some possibility of creating a sense of continuity, a persistence of vision.

Given how responsive he was to the voices of others, his favouring of the monologue as a poetic form is not surprising. Some of his finest work was written in this mode, dating back to 'The pity' at the start of *The Poet Reclining*, and reaching through to 'Wall dreams' at the close of *Shed*. This latter poem contains the allusion to 'Voices behind voices' (*Shed*, 313), a phrase which succinctly identifies one of the most distinctive features of the later monologues, and his collections more generally: just how many different voices he allowed to surface. Once again, this characteristic helped to seal his affinity with the Anglo-Saxon elegy, 'The Wanderer':

> Well it's partly because the Old English poems are so anonymous and multi-voiced that I keep coming back to them. If you actually look at 'The Wanderer' there's at least four voices in there, one of them being the Christian scribe who's writing it down and imposing his culture on it. I've looked at it very carefully and there are a series of frames and within each frame is a different voice. What I like in the poem is the fact that voices drift in and drift out and they don't introduce themselves and they don't have names. The names are not important. What's important is what the voice says. To me, that's part of the world we've lost. We've lost that collective gathering of voices. What I really seek is that collective unconscious, if you like, out of which this voice rises and falls. Bakunin: 'waves of the sea'. To me, that's the republic, the republic of voices and identities and people.[31]

'a collective gathering of voices': in talking of Smith returning to an original wound as a source of his poetry, I risk implying an inward-looking, self-obsessed poet. What I mean to suggest is that he used his continuing contact with that 'hole in the tooth' to heighten his receptivity to the dilemmas of others. He saw himself as one voice among many, a part of 'the republic of voices'.

He was well aware of the dangers of self-preoccupation, playfully caricaturing his early work in 'Departure's speech': 'Once I was a puppy, a young poetrie apprentice / in the school of Whingeing Willy's blighted adolescence' (*Shed*, 91). In 'Winter occasions', first published in 1976, he both draws attention to the issue, while exposing one means of outflanking it. Once more the male psyche is represented as a disturbed site, ghosted by violence and loss:

> In his sleep
> knives clatter, armies gather,

storms rake the upland, a girl
goes singing a love song over the watermeads...
   (*Poet Reclining*, 93)

The difference is that this narrative is told from the perspective of
a woman, a latter-day Hermione drafted in from Shakespeare's *A
Winter's Tale* and cast as a rural wife brooding on the lot she has
married, a writer who familiarly enough has his head metaphorically
'in a sling, / dragging his deaths like a whale / round with him'.
His neglect of her means that 'it's years since [she] missed him'.
She, like the image of the girl, is disappearing from his sight. That
loss, what she and the girl collectively represent, is also a critical
concern examined in other contexts in key later works, such as
'Hawkwood', Smith's penning of the imagined secret journal of a
14th century mercenary, collected in *Terra* (1986), and a number
of the interlinked poems in *Wormwood* (1987), a volume that largely
arose out of his experience of being writer-in-residence at Worm-
wood Scrubs prison for two years.

The satirical element of 'Winter occasions' presages Smith's
growing use of humour to leaven the texture of his poems. Like
changing the angle of perspective, it also allowed him to gain dis-
tance on subject-matter. In later work he became adept at modu-
lating the intensity of narrative engagement. On one level, isn't
this the lesson of *Fox Running*? After all, the key movement of the
poem is a centrifugal one, away from the protagonist's absorption in
his own pain as he gradually begins to identify with the experience
of others and see how commonplace his particular plight is. I take this
to be the point of the riddling last line. He is able to step outside
the force-field of his own hurt and move on. Silkin reads this as
when Fox 'adopts a serious voice to appraise such truths needful
for a strategy of survival: "whó all belóngs to this blóod then?"' [32]
But surely the 'serious voice' comes a few lines earlier with the
allusion to, and affirmation of, the counsel given in 'The Wanderer':
'a man...at the end forebears boastmaking // a wise man holds out'
(*Poet Reclining*, 169). The speech idiom of *Fox Running*'s last line
suggests a different tone of voice, approaching the situation from
another angle and with a greater sense of distance on what has
happened. Imagine an old timer stumbling into a bar in a Western
after the brawl or gunfight has ended and jauntily enquiring, in a
husky, bourbonised voice, 'who all belongs to this blood then?' This
scenario it seems to me is closer to the intended inference of the
poem's final moment, while underlining Smith's commitment to an
ultimately comic rather than tragic vision. Coming off the Homeric
paradigm proposed by Northrop Frye, some literary critics have

interpreted the comic mode as essentially Odysseyan, a wanderer's tale of picaresque exploits, focusing on the quest for survival rather than heroic transcendence.[33] And what is *Fox Running* but a poem about survival, about a man coming to see the apparent disorder of his life in terms of an archetypal pattern established by wanderer figures in world literature, starting to recognise the inevitable bathos in his own existence and consequent pratfalls – 'blind drunk into the orchestra' – and understanding the necessity of picking himself up, dusting himself down like any bit part player, and going on: 'a wise man holds out'.

During the 1980s and 1990s, Smith became increasingly comfortable donning a comic persona in his work. He relaxed into the role of the latter-day travelling scribe, singing for his supper, and his poetry became more accommodating and gregarious. At times, his list-making took on baroque proportions – see for example 'The Chicken Variations' or 'The Great Hat Project' (*Shed*, 196-200 & 242-46) – and such pieces were well received by the growing audience for his work. He was a marvellous reciter of his own poetry, and the last time I saw him give a reading it was his *tour de force* rendition of 'The Great Hat Project' which really kindled the audience's attention. And yet while I recognise that these poems are virtuoso displays of wit and inventiveness, I also find that the constant stream of one-liner comic observations are all virtually of the same order which ultimately dims their surprise and effectiveness. It is as though all the different jokes merge into the one gag which becomes tiring through repetition. I also recognise that among Smith admirers holding this belief puts me in the minority. He himself was quite unfazed by this kind of criticism. When I first got to know him I unfortunately lacked the gumption to refrain from offering my considered opinion on the matter, and amazingly he always took it in good part. For me, the strongest of his later sequences are invariably those in which by some means 'restraint and excess interact with each other'.[34]

The formulation is Alan Lovell's, commenting on what he takes to be the key ingredients of many of the best recent British films, but to my mind it also holds good for Smith's work, particularly on the macro-level of overall sequences, but still on the micro-level of individual poems and even sections of poems. In the 1998 sequence, 'Wire through the heart', for instance, written after a trip to the border areas separating Hungary from Slovakia and the Ukraine, there is the 'restraint' of the opening poem's *ubi sunt* lyricism: 'in some town...where is no schul any more, no Sabbath, / no dark sidelocked men arriving on carts / with their shawled

114

women, their solemn / children in long coats' ('Where the scythe has been'; *Shed*, 278), and the closing poem's careful documenting of a survivor's own story: ' "These are my blunt carpenter's hands / and this on their backs the frost / that gnawed them at Szolyva, three winters" ' ('Malenki robot'; *Shed*, 286); but there is also the 'excess' of the tongue-in-cheek skit on 'The Secret Police' (*Shed*, 280): 'So let's hear it for the secret police, / a much misunderstood minority', and the droll travelogue concerning the interminable fun to be had at the 'Border theatre' of the absurd (*Shed*, 284): 'No, I am carrying no contraband, / no firearms, Kalashnikovs, missile launchers, / no drugs, no coils of copper wire from Minsk, / no nuclear material, no body parts...' As to how this dynamic operates within individual poems, it may be worthwhile to consider the section that begins 'Think of Billy' and consists of two blocks of 12 lines in 'For the boys on the wing', *Wormwood* (*Shed*, 121). In part I have chosen this as an example because in an otherwise positive and insightful review of *Shed*, William Oxley cites the poem as an instance of Smith's 'occasionally too elliptically enjambed, thought-in-fragments poetry'.[35] Yet surely this assessment fails to appreciate the deft interlayering of voices and registers within the poem. Beneath flip, throwaway remarks a hinterland of memory and emotion opens out. Reading through this section, it is as though we descend from streetwise repartee to basement-level bluntness and pained recognition.

After a casual but loaded reference to Billy – 'He'll not wince / past the checkout' – we pass on to the figure of John, whose difficulties are initially presented in a racy, knockabout patter, one wisecrack stacked on top of another: 'Think of John / overdue in the remembering department / in the red to the last lost quid / hidden in his shoe and that owing / to Veiled Threats Associates.' This then abruptly gives way to an intense, imagistic memory of a seascape, where the implicit emphasis on space and freedom is made all the more charged and ironic by John's present circumstances: 'He recalls / a whole ocean cut to a wind and two blues.' Up to this point it has been a third person account, but the portrayal of loss seemingly quickens the narrator's own, a narrator which the poem as a whole invites us to think of as Smith himself. The emotional distance shortens, the tone becomes increasingly urgent and the alliterative measure more insistent. There's a fusion of perspectives and voices. The identity of the narrative voice in the lines that follow is blurred, though the strength of feeling is sharpened: 'He has pictures to prove it: the hills, / the harebells whipped by the first / wind of September.' Finally, becoming the focal point of the merged grief, a nameless woman is addressed in the first person and in a plain style speech which, in the last line in particular, feels ground out: 'Love I remember: / you were fierce, you persisted / through whatever the weather was.'

After the break, the next two lines pull back slightly from this level of intensity, while at the same time wittily subverting the lexis of hope offered by both organised religion and classical literature. Popular evangelical teaching is ironised and an anthology-line by John Donne inverted: 'Born again to the wind's tap on brick. / Born again to the island of the self'. By now, though, the jokes seem increasingly caustic, and they suddenly darken into a nightmare imagery, reminiscent of Fox's worst moments: 'the same giggle in the orchestra pit, / nights when the snake of her dark voice / slides over me'. The emotional load again momentarily lightens, though not the thematic bleakness, when the woman's barbed aphorism is played off against pop music's banal pronouncements on affairs of the heart: 'She says all journeys / have no returns. The radio sings / *She & I don't go to the laundrette no more.*' The section draws to a close with a comic self-portrait by the narrator, the botched appellation, 'Orfus', a.k.a. Orpheus, a carnivalesque moment of excess suggesting a cartoon replacement of the lauded original. There is even a hint of paronomasia, an awful pun, Aw Fuss or even All Fuss, which as it acknowledges – nudge/wink – Smith's presumption to be 'such a heavy breather down the line to intensity', as Peter Porter designated him,[36] and mocks his aspiration to be able to navigate his way through such dark subject-matter, nonetheless also signals his kinship with this terrain of lost voices through the sudden restraint of the diction and the flattened-out rhythm of the final three lines: 'I'm Orfus / the man who has everything calling back / from the border and lost her forever, / bringing no light back from the dead'.

Perhaps unsurprisingly, there was in Ken as a person something of that same duality of excess and restraint, expansiveness and reserve. I remember once setting off down Barking Road in East Ham with him to get a pizza and coming close to passing out with thwarted expectation as he proceeded to flamboyantly greet someone or other every two or three yards. I also remember a three-hour car journey of silence. I remember calling at his house one morning only for him to appear at the doorstep like a cross between a magician and someone out of a Homepride Flour advert, a great plume of plaster dust wafting out from behind him. It transpired that the previous night he had taken a notion to knock down an upstairs inner wall using his father's billhook and a mallet. As can be imagined, his partner, the poet Judi Benson, was not best pleased and I think we were shamelessly used to coax her downstairs to say hello to the visitors who had travelled all the way from Yorkshire. By the evening, over a meal of garlic lightly flavoured with lamb, he was in great form – all stories and fun. He could be irritable, sometimes seemed restless, but one of my dominant impressions of Ken was his gentleness. On the one or two occasions he visited, he was happiest just pottering around the garden, seeing what was and was not coming on, comparing notes. His feel for and knowledge of features of the natural landscape was very strong, and this goes some way to explaining his ability to evoke their presence so sharply in his work.

In Moira Conway's photograph of Ken from the mid-80s, he stares out from the shadow cast by the brim of a fedora and over a pair of tinted glasses. The gaze is steady, hard. You would not like to mess with this man. But that is just it. It's a look, a guise, one more ruse in his own great hat project: poetrie pup turned tough guy. Ken's most formidable poetry was written by staying in close contact with his own sharp sense of vulnerability. His courage as a writer was to continually push himself physically and mentally into those regions that quickened his senses and stimulated his imagination – 'gone into everything he is scared of', is how the journeyman's role is represented in his sequence, 'The Wanderer Yakob' (*Shed*, 105). As he journeyed through a late 20th century world of congested urban conurbations in the West and disputed sectors of land in the East of Europe, a delight in what was new, strange, or 'off the wall' was always shadowed by an apprehension of menace and the presentiment of death. He seems to have courted this atmosphere as much as he feared it. An admirer of Lorca, it allowed him to draw the presence of *duende* into his poetry. The following excerpt from 'As it happens', a poem set in and around London, especially Wormwood Scrubs, reveals a sensibility far from comfortable with, and yet captivated by, the menace it apprehends:

> The lift shrieks
> at the seventeenth floor in the air shaft
> the wind hunts ruins to howl through,
> the doors open on blue video voices.
>
> You hear glass split, long clatter of heels
> on the stairwell, a man's shout and a slam
> all the way to the street where a car
> coughs like a baby.
>   Later you hear
> through the breezeblock *it's not her*
> *car as it happens, it's not his baby.*
>
>   ('in the flats, flat voices'; *Shed*, 113)

There's a listing here once again, a juxtaposing of intimidating and enigmatic sound fragments suggesting their own ominous, gapped narrative.

Though it may seem a banal remark, sound references became an increasingly important aspect of Ken's poetry. Commenting on his work, Sean O'Brien has argued that he 'discarded much of the image-based practice of English poetry'.[37] To an extent this is true, though Smith remained someone who very much worked through his senses, only it was often the aural rather than the visual detail which he recorded. As the above extract shows, he was acutely aware of sounds, noise, particularly the day to day dissonance within contemporary societies and its impact upon individuals. The late American sequence, 'Eddie's other lives', collected in *Wild Root*, focuses on just this concern. This is from 'Noises off':

> And there is always racket, machinery
> that bleeps to say your dinner's done,
> your laundry's dry, horns, talking trucks,
> the chatter of the video arcades
> and the low murmur of the soaps
> and the endless wailing of the cops.
>
> (*Shed*, 219)

The truculent excess of this catalogue means that the narrator is cast as the archetypal companion to avoid in a bar, but again the humour is pointed. Noise is seen as something other than simply a physical phenomenon of the environment. Eddie's ability to orientate himself, to find a clear map-sense, is frustrated by corporate America's acoustic overload. There is a scattering of focus, a vitiating of selfhood, and a consequent ratcheting up of anxiety. As a media concept, noise is defined as that which breaks up and distorts the flow of communication. As a poet, Ken is interested in that which breaks up and distorts people's meaningful interaction with the world around them. He possessed a remarkable acuity for the static jamming people's lives, arresting growth and inhibiting a sense of wonder. It is in this respect that he is a poet of both physical and semantic noise – psychological noise, cultural noise, political noise, noise that cuts across and fragments an individual's life. And not just in the West: the ideological noise, for example, of the Soviet army summarily dragging wire across a street in 1944 to divide Slovakia from the Ukraine, and in the process cutting a man's existence in half. In 'Malenki robot' we read how he can 'take a walk / down to the border and look back / into the other world' he has always known only yards away but which is now seemingly lost forever.

A comparatively late piece by Ken, 'Wall dreams', collected in *Shed* (313-19), serves to draw together a number of ideas broached in this essay. The poem quickly becomes basically the monologue of a quintessential Smith Everyman figure – a Roman squaddie patrolling the border region of Hadrian's Wall. Behind this voice, however, presences and moments from earlier texts flicker and move. Nowhere is this palimpsest quality more apparent than in a closing section of the poem, which begins with an emphatic listing of the essential geographical features: 'Scarp. Ditch. Crag.' As in other works, the revenant of the Old English line, consonant heavy – 'blue cap of the sky, cloud splattered' – gathers momentum and runs-on through a welter of sounds and impressions: 'mountains of mist / shuttering the hills, sliding over / my eye corners as I run, bearing / my message, sheep voicing / their complaints, bull braying'. The narrator finds himself one tale among many – 'Voices behind voices' – as he tracks a clearing of vision, lingering on a childhood memory through the change in pace conjured by a series of open vowels: 'Where was / my beginning, my eyes opening / to the foggy river banks, woods, / wide snakey water lands'. But any semblance of a clear connection with the past is lost, broken; something other stares back at him now: 'glimpse / of my own stranger's face / in the moonlit pool at midnight'. The world's noise sharpens its pitch, a sense of menace closes in, and still he presses on, the closely battened phrasing also registering an undiminished will to enquire: 'cries of the flayed ox, the stuck pig, / flogged horse, dogs hunting / along the horizon's line, always?' Not for the first time in Ken's poetry, into this scene of male violence strays the visitation of a grieving female embodying another sound, another way of being, one almost impossible to fathom in the surrounding mêlée: 'Someone who sang to me, / a woman, milk and tears flowed from her.' Yet despite everything, the poem closes with the narrator celebrating his existence, celebrating life, in this 'lost world': 'I am in praise. Of the sun. Of the bear, the wolf, the deer. / I am in praise of the horned god that hunts them all. / I am in praise of all that breathes.' The last line in this catalogue is hard to bear now for all those who loved Ken and his work. A marvellous kinetic writer, a motion poet in many senses, stilled. But not his vision. That will persist and run on.

No doubt in writing this essay I've simply produced my own barrage of noise. In trying to highlight a few key elements in his poetry and pave the way for the letter extracts and interview which follow, I've risked making it sound more one-sided and darker than it really is. I've obscured subtleties and whole areas of his work, I know. Yet it was because his apprehension of encroaching noise was so keen that his representation of what he termed the 'gracenotes' was all the more poignantly realised.[38] They often appeared in telling relief. As one small example, there is the delicate poise of this quiet celebration of care and love. The wanderer is home from his travels, in the presence of all that he finds healing, and open to the small acts, the small details, that still for him make the world radiant:

> My love consoles me. Sometimes I think of her,
> a bird high in the tree of the house, a river
> of sunlight warm on her cheeks.
>
> So much patience with paint, silk, *the least gap*
> *and it bleeds*. In the end it's a scarf in the wind, love,
> beads of water scattered into sunlight.
>
> ('The afternoon'; *Shed*, 311)

My correspondence with Ken was irregular, but included two very long letters he sent in response to questions I had put to him. In June 1987 I was completing an MA at Sheffield University and my final piece of work was on Ken's poetry. He was, as ever, extraordinarily generous with his time. Essentially, he used my queries as useful prompts for his own musings, often breaking free of the boundary of a particular enquiry and making the agenda his own. The result is a candour and depth of response which is sometimes hard to achieve in recorded interviews. His account of how 'The Eli Poems' came to be written, for example, is a fascinatingly intimate record. As a discussion of poetic crafting, of the pressing personal imperatives that can lie behind stylistic and narrative decisions, it is absorbing. What follows is an edited version of these two letters.

The last time I spoke to Ken was in the summer of 2002 when I phoned to congratulate him on the radio broadcast of 'My Father Fading Out', a series of poems with biographical prose links, focusing on his relationship with his father. I was struck at the time by the description of his father arriving in Hull in 1937 with little more to his name than a few odds and ends tucked into 'a small brown attaché case'. The detail reminded me of a picture by the Scottish artist Jack Vettriano, entitled 'The Drifter', showing a man dressed *circa* the 1930s arriving alone at a coastal shoreline with just such a case in his right hand. I sent him a copy of the image, which he really liked, and then a small book featuring Vettriano's paintings. Perhaps he saw something of both himself and his father in that portrait. Perhaps he envisaged himself picking up that case and continuing on with the journey, only this time the case resembled one of those exemplary travellers' display chests he mentions in the following letters. I don't know. But if this piece of fancy were true, then that case/chest would contain the product of his trade, poems such as 'Family group', 'The pity', 'The Wild Rose', 'The Eli Poems', *Fox Running*, 'Hawkwood', 'As it happens', 'The Shadow of God' and 'Wall dreams', a body of work that makes Ken Smith one of the great post-war English writers. Quite soon after sending the book, I received a card back from Ken, our last real communication, which read:

> Thanks so much for the Vettriano book. Wow! Dirty romantic, neo-lowlife. Love it.
>
> Off to the Balkans 21st – Macedonia, Montenegro, all the way up the coast, via Split, Dubrovnik, etc. Her indoors joins me in Trieste and then we'll go to Slovenia.
>
> Life of Reilly.

Ken Smith in Sarajevo with microphone, 2002.

TWO LETTERS FROM KEN SMITH

Leeds: the clumsy apprentice

Amongst the many things I learned from Silkin in what was essentially an apprenticeship to a trade was very close, careful, attentive, observation...Through working with him I was fortunate to be in at the birth of the flower poems, and able to observe him working them from initial notion to finished sequence.[39] But I don't think I was trying to do any more than that in those early poems that were contemporaneous with his flower poems. He was, I wasn't, seeking to suggest their proximity to human doings. I was far too clumsy an apprentice for that, and was drawn more towards the emblematic and therefore the question of anthropomorphism until finally, bored, I set myself against that sort of essayish writing, where the comparisons were often suspect, and where, in fact, it was my holding back to a structured approach that inhibited them. So this is mainly why they didn't go into *The Poet Reclining*, and I feel much the same way towards them now. Neil Astley had to argue me into including some of them, if only for the sake of representation, but I think if I'd had it all my own way I'd have dropped most of them.

Exeter: moving beyond the lyric

I moved from Leeds to Exeter in the summer of '65. I stopped writing for a while, and the whole business of moving threw things, and me. I missed the north, and couldn't get used to Devon and the absence of declared warmth such as I'd come to take for granted in Leeds, didn't much like the place, but found myself living at the back of extensive woods called Stoke Woods, and spent a lot of time up there getting lost. Hence the poem 'The Wood', much of its imagery, and the sort of ruminations provoked therein. I was trying for something larger than the short peroration on a fossil etc (the poetry of 'framed observations', says Garfitt).

I think I was beginning to think what I still think, that we begin in the lyric, but there's a limit to the lyric, happy or sad, the range of moods involved, the things that can be said, and in any case there's a limit to youthful effusions because there's a limit on youth. The question is how to get over this hump, to the other more complex forms of the narrative and the dramatic. Some poets don't. I'm not sure that Keats lived long enough to do so, find Wordsworth very boring once he got through with the lyric, love the return to it in Yeats, suspect that Thomas drank himself out because he couldn't get beyond it (he despised the drama he did for BBC). I am embarrassed by this poem, and find it clumsy, but I think it is the beginnings of several directions – the want to write the long poem, or something sustained beyond the page's turning, a want for scale and scope beyond the lyric and my boredom with still lives, a want for things to move and happen in the poem.

America: a new beginning

There was a long silence after *The Pity*, which meant I hadn't written much since 'The Wood', in '66, but for a few poems in the first section of *Work, distances*. I think I was fading out, writing less, settling down to being a nice lib studies teacher in Exeter College of Art, and so eventually I reacted, and got myself kicked out of that and went to the States. So there I am in '69, in Pennsylvania. The States was a great charge, and for a while it was exciting to discover other ways of writing a poem than the old banging on of the English, hence Bly, Wright, and the translations available through the Sixties Press. After a while England, and ways English, ceased to be for me. At the same time I didn't much take to America, which was in Vietnam etc, and is a pretty coarse society, but I got interested in Indians, and in the discontinuity that America both gains and loses from. Exile became a theme, and yes I could identify, and yes I could express inner exile, or alienation, through exile as a metaphor. The Rothenberg books,[40] and a whole slew of interest in 'the primitive' unquote, were part of my investigation then.

For about 4 years I cut myself off from England and things English, from Europe and European ways of thinking, and though I didn't much identify with America either, I took what I wanted from the supermarket. I became a lot more open, I guess; it was the tail end of the 60s, and I'm a slow learner, but suddenly there was a sense of a new beginning, that many things considered not possible could be reconsidered. At the same time I realised, heavily, that I was stranded, with 3 kids and wife, far from anywhere, and without any means of getting back to where I'd come from. Then I thought, but where was that? Devon or Yorkshire? And then I realised there isn't any place called base, or home, or the centre. The centre of the universe is wherever (for me) I happened to be, and my business was to get us all out of a hole (Slippery Rock, Pa),[41] hold the ship together through hostile terrain, and otherwise be wherever. I realised also that the only way on was through the writing, and thereafter I relaxed.

Mask voices

'Song for the whites' [42] – well, here I was doing what I've often enough done since: using a mask voice for my own, so the voice has two ways to go – the public meaning of the Indian, the dignified survivor; the private language of my own voice in my own situation. I felt myself among strangers, words too complex, and back there (England) a mouthful of ashes (charity's ashes and lemon juice, somewhere, which came from a report from the Biafran famine); I had found a way to use my own voice and what I felt through an undelineated persona...The 'Minnesota' poem came along with the 'Song for the whites'; in fact a lot of these all at a gulp. 'Crying woman' seemed to move things along a little bit: not the statement about a feeling, but the feeling, more a chanting than a disquisition, closer to what I was after [...]

Two things occur to me: one is that for me it was a new departure as a way of using words, and seemed to get away from the English formulation of language into sensible grammatical units all full of meaning to be unravelled. It was a departure, a flight, and seemed to me a breakthrough, and part of what I had gone away from England to try to get away from. The second point I'm less sure of, but I have a feeling that having written that poem I was sort of ready for the Eli poem, that that sort of departure made the Eli poem possible. Not sure what I'm at here, but I think there's a case for writing one thing to make another possible, or bring it closer.

Reaching through to Kate

['The Eli Poems' sequence] is linked (I was conscious of it) with poems like the 'Killhope Wheel' and Wainwright's '1815', with moments in Hill's Mercian poems (the woman making nails, for instance),[43] but I think all these are rooted back into industrial memory, which was still strong around Leeds and the West Riding 20 years back, and probably still is, and they probably all derive from our readings of E.P. Thompson and the work of the Hammonds – *The Town Labourer, The Village Labourer, The Bleak Age*.[44] These latter, by the way, were in my mind I know when I wrote 'The Wood' [...]

At the time I was more than anything else afraid – of the dreams as they overlapped into waking life, of a waking life that seemed as much invaded by Eli as was sleep. Think of mathematical sets overlapping. In this case my belief in the existence of Eli and of Kate, that they had lived, or that they or something of them lived still, or lived in my own genetic memory, or that they were djib-huks who invaded me. Whatever their origin, I believed in their reality, its projection onto me, and recall making a decision that all I could do was project them out again, in the only way I knew how, in poems, or at any rate in writing. To transmit them, but as an act of self defence. Eli was very threatening. It felt that what he demanded was that I move out of the way, that I stop being, in order to allow him to communicate with her, and that she was in some way 'sleeping' in me [...]

What little I perceived of Kate was that she was wounded, that she didn't want to hear his apologies for deserting her to die in childbirth with his child for the sake of his marriage, nor his continuing declarations of love for her. I felt I also had to protect her from him, that she was not ready to wake, but that these two were still tied to each other and neither could be free without she learned of his grieving. My task was to transmit this message to her, somewhere in myself [...]

Perhaps what came to bother, and ultimately to comfort, me were the similarities in the narrative of Kate and Eli with my father's life (born in Ireland, mother died in childbirth) and the fact of his death, so that the narrative seemed pointed at me. I couldn't have known what it was warning me of, but I felt endangered, and the real event and the dream narrative seemed linked. Then I realised I had to write something, a form of exorcism perhaps, though it meant going further in to find out more (the fool in his folly), and having written the initial dreamed poem, 'Eli's poem', I then sat down to consciously try to write. Nothing much came. Then I had the idea to try automatic writing, but since my writing method has always been with a keyboard nothing came of that till I tried it on the typewriter (typing but not looking at it). Well, nothing came of that malarkey either, but what came into my mind very clearly was the image of Kate in the marshy landscape, and then 'The marsh' poem. She was, I think, going to the place where she would die.

I can't remember the order much after that, but suspect it may be in the order that I have them in, with the exception of the Eli poem itself, so that all the rest was written to understand more of that first poem. 'The third month' was intended to be like a 3rd person account, neighbourhood gossip if you like. So then I had a description of her and her predicament, her story, receding into reportage, and this picked up again later in the 'What was done' poem, protagonist, villain, and chorus. I realised I had only written about her, whereas for Eli, who was the bothersome one, I had written 1st person singular how he felt. Trying to get to her, he always came in the way, so I decided then to try to speak more clearly his feelings for her, to reach her by way of his lament. I was after him, not with the desperate voice of the 'Eli poem', nor with the bragging public voice that others heard of him, but the man inside him who must have loved her, made love to her, shared tenderness with her, and this, later, he realised, he had not only lost but betrayed, even destroyed. 'The rooming house' and 'The lament' came together and are more or less continuous as his inner voice, his memory, though I think there is a sort of progression from his voice to mine ('all my effort/ to release you'); I have a feeling that the mask and the voice come close together here.

Now, amongst the things I was thinking was a visit, some years before, that Silkin and I made together to Haworth parsonage – not so much the house as the churchyard and the countryside around it. I recall walking up on to the moor and talking to some roadmen, one of whom talked of the bogs men and cattle had been lost in, once he said, a horse and cart went down. Maybe he was bullshitting me, it barely matters; one or both of us believed him. So I drew on that landscape and background, though you can add in much of Yorkshire and Dartmoor too. However, in the churchyard there we were reading the histories of families buried together – many dead in childbirth, many women dead of childbirth, some stones where the old man was eventually buried on top of two wives who'd died young and umpteen dead infants, and Silkin and I both realised how powerfully for these people, in all their puritanism, sex and death were linked. So this thought was in my mind in these two laments, and the thought that the link should not lessen the intensity of either, either.

How these two relate to the rest of the sequence were that, having tended to Eli's feelings, I could tend then to my own, and hence 'The obsession' in which the I is me, my obsession with this narrative, with these two, in particular with her. I realised that in my attempts to write about her (in any attempt) I falsified, fictionalised, her, accepting that the real Kate could never fully be come at, 'I have shaped you in words that aren't true / in my dream you move as you would not move'. For this poem I went way back to an old dream, a recurring nightmare of the ridge, the deserted house, of someone, not really me, searching through musty cupboards and drawers for something. I had never been able to account for it, but I had always woken up inexplicably terrified from it. If I accepted one possible scenario or explanation, it was Kate returning to the place she had died in, looking for her child. Deciding to do so for the space of the poem, I wrote the obsession out, but I couldn't get to it till I'd gone through him, those two poems of the rooming house and his lament. In the inner, unexplained narrative, he kept a lodging house in which Kate lived; he was her landlord. He'd casually seduced her, gotten her pregnant, and only later realised that what he had was more than mere sex, and what he'd been the cause of [...]

'What was done'? I think that's 3rd person reporter, gossip again, voices blending in with my own, reportage, a more 'balanced' way of reporting the events in intimate detail made possible by having gotten through the other poems in the sequence. So this is like a running down of the intensity, and then I really thought I'd finished, and then I wrote 'The door' piece – later rewritten to try to provide a clearer background narrative.[45] About a year later, having moved now to Massachusetts, the 'Half songs' quite suddenly burst on me. I think I told you – I was vacuuming the floor, alone in the house, and as I turned I thought for an instant I actually saw her, wan and dressed in a flowery sort of green, turning away, but with her face turning towards me in some acknowledgement. I felt she was awake, "realised", and that she was going away, and I wrote that poem very quickly. It's my voice, but remoter, a little more abstract, a little more the voice of memory or rumour or history. Then I felt free of it all [...]

More and more over the years I've come to accept Kate as an anima figure who behaved as Jung describes such figures – they press forward and become more defined, they demand attention. Eli then is my own resisting animus, the dark shadow that comes along with her; if such figures are not allowed to be realised, they break out anyway, and I rather suspect that a lot of the men I've been dealing with in prison represent the underside of this process: the anima takes over, or they seek to destroy it, or become psychotic, murderous or suicidal, or both. These thoughts are more tentative, and represent where I am now feeling my way as ever. To understand all this from this or that psychology is however for me only one of several, and some conflicting, methods, tools, measures, explanations, scenarios. But I'd like to dare hope that since her release I have acknowledged and drawn from her side of myself more than before. Frail as she may have been then.

Equally, and I don't think this conflicting as a scenario, I have speculated on the narrative as some sort of genetic inheritance, and wondered what of memory we might carry from generation to generation. I have no scientific basis for this thought, only my strong conviction some times it seems so. Perhaps the idea of patterns or sets helps here; maybe this particular set of coincidences, overlappings of the pattern as to childbirth, etc, means a similarity of circumstance draws on an existing pattern or encourages the psyche to provide one. The incidence of my father dying takes me to further mystery, since there's a time element involved, and the disturbances more or less ceased when he died (i.e., they preceded it).[46] I don't know what to make of this, other than to wonder about time, and whether it's only human perception that renders it a one way flow.

The clearing

In '72 I managed at last to get us out as far as Massachusetts, where I had a poet job for a year, a very fine year indeed.[47] Near where we lived in Worcester there were extensive woods again where I often went, and these animulae poems are from there. Around then I was reading a lot of Merwin amongst other things. One day I was up there with a student of mind, an Indian, a man who taught me a hell of a lot, most of it impossible to repeat though much of it simple woodcraft and how to get around in the woods. We were watching a hawk circling, waiting for it to dive, for a long time. It didn't. It went straight up and we never did see it come down.

I had a dog in those days, and he and I (I came to realise) had worked out a range in the woods, mostly around the area of an abandoned farm, the land going back to wilderness. Beyond the limits of the range things got dark and hostile. This was the clearing. I learned to let be there, and one day quite dramatically broke through. At the moment of it, I found a stick (I still have it) and the broken off end was a wolf's head, and I thought it winked. There was also a hawk configuration in it, and a real hawk in the trees that was out of breath in the way the crows had declared on it. I wrote Hughes about it all, but he wrote back to say it was a misinterpreted icon, or some such. I wasn't and aren't trying to interpret this and other moments there. I went back there, about ten years later, and found it was the same: the only place I've ever found where the natural world did not flee from my being there.

Too primal?

Well, I dunno about Porter and being too primal.[48] He's a good critic, I think, and I don't mind being the heavy breather down the line to whatever it is. In America I became loose, and have never quite been able to glue myself back into the ordered English landscape. Porter's a classicist, but a respectable one, and much of what I've said here would be tosh to him. In the poems I think I've come more to say what I think is and less to seek to interpret it. How is this reductive? What I feel is that there are whole ranges of feeling that we deny ourselves, or are denied us, and what I want is recognition of them, exploration of them, which sounds to me like more, not less. When poetry is boiled down to irony and wit and intellectual reflection and precise observations, then I think it is reductive. Or have I misunderstood the relation primal/reductive? Perhaps I stress the commonality of human feeling? But what I hope to stress is its depth and range.

Back to England, Exeter: the wanderer's ways

A pitfall is egocentricity, and the solipsist marshland where nothing can be said, or where the I in the poem dwarfs the perceptions in the poem. Hence the reshaping, recasting, of my own experience to blend it with another, historical or imaginary, a persona that changes but is usually some variant of the wanderer. I'm bored with Tony's poems about his dead father,[49] and the particulars don't include but exclude, and what I'm after is (I hope) more universal, and therefore the mythic element. We're each of us if you like our own myth, and that myth to be measured against the mythic. Does this make sense? Narrative, because that's the best way of structuring, and length requires it. Fable, because fable, the element of strangeness, for I find even the mundane and ordinary quite strange. In some ways, perhaps, I'm reaching back to the world I knew in childhood (not necessarily to childhood) that was fabulous, or fabled, contained mystery, and an oral culture back there in the dale's length. We believed that a black flag in the fire meant the arrival of a stranger, and all sorts of funny stuff. It may have had no meaning but I miss it still, and think our urban sensible lives suffer from such absences.

So I like, and fear, signs, coincidences, serendipities. Visiting a mate of mind who lives in a shitty towerblock in Silvertown, as I was leaving in the paranoia-inducing twilight of the district, there in the corner of the entrance to the building was an old man, a traveller, a man with a grindstone who had laid out all his sharpened knives. It wasn't him who said I put an edge to an edge but another man I met in Pennsylvania, an engineer with a box of sharp tools; and neither was the man with the omens. But I put them together, in a clatter of violent and dangerous images [...][50]

I'm very interested in chance, in coincidence, in random, in ways of seeing things side-on or from an odd angle, or putting apparently disparate elements together. I like finding: things, words, images. I consider that the patterns of the world are stranger than our science considers, but am encouraged to think so by developments in physics, and think some thoughts are like very long radio waves, and take a time to think themselves out [...]

Tristan.[51] Yes a conscious reaction to events in my own life, a correspondence...the Tristan and Isolde narrative seemed a useful vehicle within which to conceal it all, and univeralise it too. As for source I really had only the vaguest grasp of them: readings around the Arthurian canon, some version or other of the T&I mythos that seemed to fit and suited me to use. I think I had some precedent, or felt some, in the Kate and Eli poems. But my sources were as ever not researched in the proper sense of the word, and I found I had misremembered some of them...What I wanted was the barest outline of the tale, a compacting if you like, and more that mishmash of beliefs that popular versions of a tale compact... Most of the echoes are to the Exeter bk, if only because it was there and available. Hence in my mind there are real images of real places: 'men leaning on the cathedral stones'. Centuries after, you can see where they leaned.

That said, the sequence took on a life of its own, and amongst the various voices I was trying from all three corners of the eternal triangle, a more central voice seemed to emerge through the writing. The voice that comes out, by number 10 say, is more or less my voice, me speaking on a good day, but more a voice based on my voice, pitching one way off the language and the other through whatever remote similarities there might be between events in my own life and events in the poem. I have a sense it's a voice I'm always reaching forward to, or becoming, and that some of the poems we're talking about are the record of some learning through some change. Mrozek, I think, says we're always falling short of the poem we haven't written yet, but I think I'm more interested in the day to day business of becoming. But the poem still took on its own life, and I had a real sense of the real existence of these people – Tristan, the two Isolde's, Mark. And their universality, the repetitions of their tragic lives, everywhere and all the time, and that led me to look for one or two direct analogies [...]

I'm very attracted to the old role of journeyman, scop, trouvere, scribe, teller of tales who lives by them and travels because of them. In industrial terms, pre-20th century, say, one served an apprenticeship and became a journeyman, a tradesman who went about to build shelves or paint portraits. If you were advertising this position in the *Guardian*, I guess you'd have to say the qualities required would be some sort of proof of qualifications, some experience in the trade and evidence of results, a couple of references from reliable umpires, and then some – willing to travel, quick and adaptable, etc. Especially

I like those toolchests carpenters used to carry: the box itself made of intricate jointwork, different woods, a fine object that demonstrates the skills of its maker, when an apprentice.

I think the storyteller has always existed, and is an essential component of society. We look for strangers to bring us news of elsewhere, to tell us tales, to entertain us and to teach us something. But the point about the storyteller is that he/she is also an outsider in some ways. Whether as a wanderer from place to place, or as recluse or someone drawn apart, or merely an inner thinker, that sort, the storyteller has to have another place to go to. Maybe what Neruda said, in that film the other week, to the postman – to write poetry you first must learn how to walk. Walk and talk, since the rhythm stimulates the thinking. For the Greeks this was the peripatetic method, I do believe.

Fox and the naked Victorians

Foxy. There is – again – an inner narrative only known to me, suppressed into the poem, and part of its invisible structure. In the final drafts of the poem I inserted a few clues, but there aren't enough, and I'm not sure it matters. It's what Fox feels rather than his story that matters, and his tale therefore exists in barest outline – that universalising bus again. So the question is, is he dead or alive, and what was going on on the tube that day? Ok: as he's wandered the city he's fallen into the delusion (or it's reak) that he keeps seeing himself going in the opposite direction, up the down escalator, glimpsed in the mirror. Or is it his double? One day when he sees him he pursues him around the underground, only to see him caught up in a riot, killed. He swaps identity, wallets, with him. So what? He has his problems now. By being 'dead' he writes off his own, but he's only stepped into the mirror, where the only difference is he parts his hair on the other side. That's all. Poem's over now, the story not worth articulating. 'But I've seen him' because he is still alive, and in the further sense 'I've seen him' in many men around the city. His tale is an everyman's, then, and either he comes to terms with it or not. Implication is he does – those latter images of him are calmer, a man of whom they say 'he's done his time' […]

The man bouncing a ball in *Fox* is from the sequential photography of Eadweard Muybridge, several of which are men and women running, batting a ball, etc. He was studying movement, but induced a friend at the university of Pa – a staid and upright German professor – to shed his clothes and bounce a ball around. That struck me as funny, and the thought that here were naked

Victorians, and that these events recorded by Muybridge were among the first attempts to provide the future (us for instance) with pictures of what it was like then, in the same place. In part it's a structural device, for the poem is long enough to go beyond being sustained by its inner narrative, and I felt the need for some firmer battening round the back of it.

The business of perception via Muybridge's photography, the fact the retina can be tricked into seeing continuous motion where is a series of still pictures run at the precise speed for all these movies to take place, this all fascinates me, and helps demonstrate the limited nature of our perception, and was intended to fall in with my theme, Fox's search for continuity in the midst of disruption and discontinuity. The corollary of taking away the standing orders of the world is further loss, alienation, possible madness, where there is no centre to the perceptions – or no continuum, no stability – the ego falls into itself, babbling, and becomes the only referent and centre, and is equally deficient. Without an outer referent of belief – mythic or philosophical or religious, other experience against which to measure itself – without in Fox's case the conti-nuities of mundane domestic life, the self falls in and becomes in one way or another quite balmy. So there's why *the persistence of vision*, as this retinal facility is known, but here I'm using it as a metaphor of the further sort of vision.

Dürer's Knight

Hawkwood. The Dürer engraving is a portrait of St Jerome in his Study. When you look at it look also at the two companion pieces the Misericorde, and Knight Death and the Devil. The three are related over a period of time, and he was working with them as sequence, as a triptych. The way of action (the Knight), the way of thought (the Misericorde, the caballic on the tower spells the date of his (recent) mother's death), the way of contemplation. I think there's no doubt which he favoured. What I have done is to take the Knight and put him in the study.

All the lost boys

Wormwood. Thinking quite openly about the Jungian shadow, the dark that always accompanies the light, and that (Jung's right) may not be ignored, is part of the whole (society/the individual psyche) and contains some of what we need to know about our-selves. We are also the dark side, and no consideration of law 'n' order, society, civilisation, would be complete without wondering what civilisation does with its malcontents, with those who deny it, an area I've stumbled into where there are questions that don't have answers. Civilisation has a hole in it, a black hole perhaps through which lies another order of events.

Here are the specifics as requested.[52] The firm, or Firm, the ICF, the Inter City Firm, so called for their nifty usage of InterCity 125. West Ham supporters (my locals), smart in the head and smartly dressed, skinhead element, NF associations, very nasty. Graffiti quite common for them, as for various Posse gangs, which are black. Some are just kids goofing off, some are into specific stuff like breakdancing, some are bad boys. D Wing houses several members of a former Southwark gang who called themselves 'Rape Posse'; less hostile graffiti testifies to the existence of the Dancehall Posse, etc. The Snipers no longer exist; they were an East London mob based on Canning Town and the docks just along from here, mostly in the late teens early twenties through to thirties age group. Robbery, etc, burglary and ripoff and (usually directed) violence their trades; effectively they were the recruiting gang for the heavy mobs, the Krays in particular, their client labourforce of runners, hitmen, mob-handers and alibi establishers. Beneath them the kids in the 14–18 bracket were the Little Snipers (poetic licence on silver, for Silver-town, pace), and they still exist. Undirected, desperate, and without any idea how far they can go, they knock over old ladies, squeeze jiffy juice in the eyes, or mob a shop or a pub in broad daylight.

You see I think the Middle Ages never ended, and Hawkwood would have been at home in the East End. The feudal structure has merely been buggered up, and we end up with nothing better: the cops took out the Krays and the Richardsons, some of whom, and the sons of some of whom, are actual members of the Scrubs' roll of dishonour. Then because about 6 years ago the little snipers made a nasty mess of a black guy they found sleeping in a ware-house on the dock, but didn't check to see he was also a biker, and an angel at that, the angels came into town and took the little snipers apart, and what they left the cops scooped up. So there's only the teenagers in their loose mob, a bit like the kids in the Lessing book, running crazy.[53] What I mean is that they're all the lost boys, they're the same people who appear later in the prison, on remand, on a short stretch, or for life.

Broken continuities

I guess all this poetry over the 25 years or so I've been at it has been the establishing of what for me is continuity, or I have to hope it is, with some consistencies through all the waverings.

Roethke in those long later mediations has images of fish getting into backwaters, side eddies that go nowhere, many metaphors of the journey,[54] and there's the picaresque to consider. Continuity is then in memory, in recall, as sharp as possible, and that not always in tranquillity, sometime in disparate and fragmentary images, because so many continuities that otherwise nurtured us through history have been broken, in our time.

The poem is initially a kind of entry in a complex cross reference system;[55] by recalling particular moments – the clearing in Massachusetts, the woods in Devon, Pa, Minnesota, Dartmoor, Cornwall, some beaches, some rivers, as close as possible to a visual print of the feel of it, I can connect with where I was then and how I felt then. Beyond this personal recording, the poem goes out seeking to find out (with Neruda) whether other people feel this, or like this, and is a running check on sanity. Beyond that, if it connects, it begins to be public property, and therefore I guess I've set out to pitch what begins in the personal into the commonality of experience, as I understand it. Therefore masks, personae, voices. Grown over that is some conscious though mostly repressed desire to voice the voiceless.

I can't bear a poetry that doesn't hammer at the wall of essential meaninglessness, if that's what it is, that doesn't test language and question perception and operate from essential and fundamental doubt. If poetry tells me what I already (think I) know, without at least questioning it, if it merely describes the describable, then I get bored. Interesting writing exists at the edge of the knowable, or the expressible, and the task of the writer (HO HO) is to push at that edge, to advance what's known, however little, and carry the light forward some way. Anyway, we live in time, and as Barthes (John) said, 'I can still hear Homer. I can still hear Chaucer. I can still hear Milton. And if I work at it, I can get to join the conversation, though I know it's only travelling one way in time'. So then there's a larger continuity, and community, of work, of reference, of readers, and of the culture. Perhaps in some ways I've begun to solve my problem, and I'm not sure what that means as regards what happens to the writing hereafter. We'll see.

NOTES

1. 'The Godfather of the New Poetry', Bloodaxe Books catalogue, 1998. This interview is reprinted below: see pp.144-45.

2. Peter Barry, *Contemporary British poetry and the city* (Manchester University Press, 2000), p.90.

3. Barry, p.89.

4. Ted Hughes, *Winter Pollen: Occasional Prose* (London: Faber, 1994), p.244.

5. Hughes, *New Selected Poems: 1957-1994* (London: Faber, 1995), pp.290-91.

6. Smith, 'A poet punching above his own weight', *Poetry London*, 44 (Spring 2003), p.44.

7. Roger Garfitt, 'Outside on the move', *Times Literary Supplement*, 24 June 1983, p.661.

8. See the publication details page of the 1981 Bloodaxe edition.

9. 'Richard Hoggart in conversation with Tony Harrison', in *Tony Harrison*, ed. Neil Astley (Bloodaxe Books, 1991), p.43.

10. Theodore Roethke, 'Some Remarks on Rhythm', in *20th Century Poetry and Poetics*, 4th edn, ed. Gary Geddes (Toronto: OUP, 1996), p.902.

11. Unpublished section of the Bloodaxe Books catalogue interview.

12. Letter to Colin Raw, 17 June 1996.

13. Ruth Padel, *52 Ways of Looking at a Poem* (London: Chatto & Windus, 2002), p. 14.

14. Smith, *Frontwards in a Backwards Movie* (Todmorden, Lancashire: Arc, 1975), collected in *A Book of Chinese Whispers* (Bloodaxe Books, 1987).

15. Letter to Ken Smith, 18 September 1972.

16. Letters to Ken Smith, 1 August and 9 September 1976.

17. Daniel Donoghue (ed.), *Beowulf: A Verse Translation*, trans. Seamus Heaney (New York: W. W. Norton, 2002), p. 242.

18. Linden Peach, *Ancestral Lines: Culture and Identity in the Work of Six Contemporary Poets* (Bridgend: Seren, 1993), p. 40.

19. Sidney Keyes, *Collected Poems* (Manchester: Carcanet, 2002). The final four lines of 'William Wordsworth' read:

> He was a stormy day, a granite peak
> Spearing the sky; and look, about its base
> Words flower like crocuses in the hanging woods,
> Blank through the dalehead and the bony face. (p.30)

Also, see the epigraph to 'The pity', *The Poet Reclining*, p.16.

20. William Wordsworth, *Selected Poetry and Prose*, ed. Philip Hobsbaum (London: Routledge, 1989), p.92.

21. Wordsworth, *Selected Poetry and Prose*, p.100. See the following stanza:

> As a huge stone is sometimes seen to lie
> Couched on the bald top of an eminence;
> Wonder to all who do the same espy
> By what means it could thither come, and whence;
> So that it seems a thing endued with sense;
> Like a sea-beast crawled forth, which on a shelf
> Of rock or sand reposeth, there to sun itself.

22. Unpublished interview with Colin Raw, 13 July 1987.

23. W.S. Merwin, *The Paris Review*, 102 (July 1987), p.73.

24. Robert Bly, *Talking All Morning* (Ann Arbor: The University of Michigan Press, 1980), p. 281.

25. Unpublished interview with Colin Raw, 13 July 1987.

26. Bloodaxe Books catalogue interview. See p.145 of this volume.

27. Letter to Colin Raw, 17 June 1996.

28. Katie Wales, *A Dictionary of Stylistics* (London: Longman, 1989), p.112.

29. See 'Peter Redgrove: The Science of the Subjective', an interview with Redgrove by Neil Roberts, *Poetry Review*, 77 no.2 (June 1987), p.8.

30. Unpublished section of the Bloodaxe Books catalogue interview.

31. Unpublished section of the Bloodaxe Books catalogue interview.

32. Jon Silkin, *The Life of Metrical and Free Verse in Twentieth-Century Poetry* (London: Macmillan, 1997), p. 342.

33. See Jonathan Bate's discussion of this area in chapter 7 of his excellent book *The Song of the Earth* (London: Picador, 2000).

34. Quoted in *An Introduction to Film Studies*, 2nd edn, ed. Jill Nelmes (London: Routledge, 1999), p. 372.

35. William Oxley, 'The self always talking to the self', *Acumen*, 44 (September 2002), p.109.

36. Quoted in *Terra* (Bloodaxe Books, 1986), p.92, Peter Porter's review of *The Poet Reclining* appeared in *The Observer*, 12 June 1983.

37. Sean O'Brien (ed.), *The Firebox: Poetry in Britain and Ireland after 1945* (London: Picador, 1998), p.207.

38. See Smith's poem 'The gracenote', *Shed*, p.252.

39. Jon Silkin's 'flower poems' were collected in *Nature with Man* (London: Chatto & Windus, 1965).

40. For example, *Technicians of the Sacred: A Range of Poetries from Africa, America, Asia and Oceania*, ed. Jerome Rothenberg (New York: Doubleday, 1968).

41. Smith was appointed Instructor in Creative Writing at Slippery Rock State College, Pennsylvania, in 1969. He held the position until 1972.

42. For the clutch of poems referred to here – 'Song for the whites', 'The Sioux cleared from Minnesota' and 'Crying woman' – see *The Poet Reclining*, pp.39-45.

43. Jon Silkin's 'Killhope Wheel' was collected in *The Principle of Water* (Manchester: Carcanet, 1974), Jeffrey Wainwright's '1815' in *Heart's Desire* (Manchester: Carcanet, 1978) and Geoffrey Hill's Mercian poems in *Mercian Hymns* (London: André Deutsch, 1971).

44. 'The Hammonds' are J.L. Hammond and Barbara Hammond, and the reference to E.P. Thompson is to his *The Making of the English Working Class*.

45. First published in *Work, distances/poems*, entitled as 'Postscript: The dead', pp. 70-71, 'The door' was heavily revised when collected in *The Poet Reclining*.

46. John Patrick Smith died on 2 April 1971.

47. Smith was Visiting Poet to Clark University, and College of the Holy Cross, both in Worcester, Massachusetts, in 1972-73. The remarks he makes here refer to poems found on pp.70-73 and 124-29 of *The Poet Reclining*.

48. This is a reference to Peter Porter's review of *The Poet Reclining*: see note 36 above.

49. See Tony Harrison's *School of Eloquence* sequence in his *Selected Poems* (London: Penguin, 1987).

50. See 'Leaving the Angel', *Shed*, p.66.

51. The sequence *Tristan Crazy* (Bloodaxe Books, 1978), was collected in *The Poet Reclining*, pp.97-107.

52. 'the specifics' are supporting background details to the gangs mentioned in the last line of 'the remembered city', part of the 'As it happens' sequence in *Wormwood*, collected in *Shed*, p.113.

53. Possibly an allusion to Doris Lessing's *The Good Terrorist* (London: Jonathan Cape, 1985).

54. See poems such as 'Meditation at Oyster River' and 'The Far Field' from Theodore Roethke's final collection, *The Far Field* (London: Faber, 1965).

55. Smith also refers to this idea in the prose piece, 'Book users' note', collected in *Burned Books* (Bloodaxe Books, 1981), pp.33-34.

THE GODFATHER OF THE NEW POETRY

Ken Smith was interviewed at his home in East Ham, London on 29 December 1997 by Colin Raw. This transcript of parts of that interview was published in the Bloodaxe Books Catalogue in 1998.

CR: Reviewers and commentators have from time to time remarked upon your lack of recognition. Have you sometimes felt yourself to be an invisible figure on the landscape of post-war English poetry?

KS: I've felt very invisible over the years and sometimes feared that I would remain invisible and sometimes didn't give a damn anyway because I think that a lot of that jostling and hyping is not really what it's about.

CR: Bloodaxe are publishing your latest collection *Wild Root* in 1998, and what links this volume, through poems such as 'Years go by' and 'No one', to your first book, *The Pity*, published in 1967, is the figure of your father. In some way or other he has featured in almost every collection you have published over the last 30 or so years. What kind of relationship did you have with him?

KS: Not very good really. He was a very bad tempered grouchy old bugger who was always losing his rag about something, so that the rows between him and my mother were constant. Eventually life just became one long battle. There were a lot of things broken and black eyes and all the rest of it. And so sometimes now, even 26 years since he died, I still dream about him. He's still there. He's still in my head. Every now and again I write a poem in which I say goodbye, this is it, get out of my head. But he always comes back. Maybe progressively over the years if I looked at those poems that are directly about that issue I might feel that he is receding, but I don't really think that he is. I think he's still in my head as alive and as bad tempered and as terrifying as he ever was.

CR: So when you're dealing with violence and aggression he's there as a presence?

KS: And as an example of a violent nature that really had no other means of expressing itself. If I could speak for him – there were also lovely aspects to him that I think I learned from. He worked with animals; he grew things. He taught me gardening. There's an image in Lawrence of his father just squatting down and staring at a flower and when I read that first years ago it twanged a string: John! There were lovely things about him. I still believe that he was illiterate, that he couldn't read or write, and I think that had a lot to do with the violence. I also have to be extremely grateful to him because although he never acknowledged his own illiteracy he made damn sure I wasn't. He made me read, he made me write things and he made me pay attention at school. He always encouraged me to get out of the hole he found himself in, because basically he was powerless. And for that I am eternally grateful.

CR: Was your sense of him as a haunted man?

KS: Haunted, but I don't know what by because he never talked about himself. He never gave any details. I didn't even know where he was born until he was dead and we got a birth certificate, which I'm still not sure to this day is actually him. John Smith, right! Well I didn't know that there was a Patrick between the John and the Smith. Nor, indeed, that he was born in Donegal and shipped over to England, aged 10, to an uncle, in inverted commas, who was just a farmer who put him to work, at the age of 10, and that he had spent his first years till then in an orphanage in Derry. I keep getting flashes, and there is a poem slowly building about it, of him with those nuns who I think were probably pretty awful.

CR: Was his taciturnity, his silence, partly responsible for drawing you back to him? Was there a sense of unfinished business?

KS: Definitely. I always imagined that there would be a conversation some day between him and me and that we would come to some understanding. Indeed, in his later years there were indications that he was mellowing and calming down, but then that was cut off because he died. So that there's also that sense of incompleteness. In a way, perhaps I'm still having this imaginary dialogue in my head with him in which, as a silent man, he never replies. So nothing has changed.

CR: You co-edited *Stand* during the 60s with Jon Silkin. He was, I take it, a critical early influence on your approach to poetry and poetry writing?

KS: Yes. He taught me a hell of a lot. He had a facility for the exhaustive critical scrutiny of a poem and I learned something of that from him. I hope I'm not as exhaustive in dismantling a poem as he was, but I think I learned to apply that critical eye and that rigour with the vocabulary of a poem, with its structure and its possibilities of meaning, from him. It was, if you think about it, an apprenticeship and I'm pretty old-fashioned. I think that whatever we are, artistically or creatively, we have to learn our trade as an apprentice in some way. Then it came time to move on and get out from under. When Silkin left Leeds for Newcastle in 1965 I headed off in the other direction, to Devon and a job there. The apprentice doesn't want to end up being a pale imitation of the master. I wanted to develop my own work and my own themes, styles, and whatever I was to do.

CR: From Exeter you moved on to America in 1969...

KS: And came back again four years later. What had struck me about being in the States was that you could be visiting writer at one institution for a year and then you've got to move on to some other place. If you've got a wife and kids and a whole truck load of furniture that's no way to live. It suddenly struck me that this was the pattern of my father's life. He was always getting the sack and everything went in a cattle-truck. Then it was a different school and a different part of Yorkshire. This was just on a bigger scale and I didn't want to do it.

CR: Presumably it was all this journeying around that encouraged your identification with *The Wanderer* of the Exeter Book?

KS: I think I became conscious of that later, when as I say after four years I was back again in Exeter. I think it was then that I focused in on the Exeter Book and the figure of the Wanderer.

CR: Both *The Wanderer* and *The Seafarer* have become key points of reference, key presences, in your work, haven't they?

KS: They're key presences, yes. The figure of the wanderer crops up again and again because it has been my condition for most of my life, but I think it is the condition for most people. As the century begins to die I think a lot of people find themselves far from their starting points or always moving on somewhere else. A phrase that came into my mind when I was doing something the other day and kept repeating itself until I finally wrote it down was 'the kinless wanderer'. I don't know what I'm going to do with it. He's still there. He's an emblematic figure.

CR: And the poems' language?

KS: Well, I love the Anglo-Saxon, I really do. I love the sound of it. I call it guttural music.

CR: Have you consciously attempted to pitch your voice in a similar manner?

KS: Yes, I have. I use the alliteration quite a lot. I use the caesura as a pause in the middle of the line quite a lot. I tend to use metaphor and not simile. I don't say one thing is like another; I try to bang them together by being another, which I think is a tendency within Germanic languages, particularly Anglo-Saxon.

CR: So you're drawn to that harsh, abrasive note?

KS: I think it's probably because it's akin to the dialect of North Yorkshire, it's the dialect of my childhood, which I haven't entirely lost though it's a long way away. When I studied Anglo-Saxon at Leeds I struggled with it for a time and then one day I suddenly thought it sounds like, '*Here lad. Go get yon bucket a' water.*' It has that clipped, guttural sound. So I did it in the voice of my childhood and I began to understand the language. It became transparent.

CR: Besides giving you access to the intimacies and emotions of that first world, is it also a means of bypassing more conventional locutions and thus responses?

KS: There's that. I agree with that. It's also that I tend to avoid the Latin words. I tend to avoid the abstract words. What I like is the concrete image for things and Anglo-Saxon provides that all the time. So I'm consciously trying to circumvent the circumlocutions in language that tend to make it mean nothing at all.

CR: That wish to get away from circumlocution fell very much in line with the kind of poetry someone like Robert Bly was advocating during the 60s: a simplified syntax to facilitate associative leaps and contact with deep images.

KS: All of that I like. It drew me to American poetry of that time: Wright, Bly, Merwin, Stafford, Haines. Landscapes that were clear. Images that were complex but there was a concrete base to them. The leaps around the imagination, the poem not confined to its simple subject-matter. This appealed to me very much. It seemed to me to open rather than close possibilities. A lot of my early work was closed, static frames around an object. Little portraits, still lives. I didn't want that any more. So American poetry of that period and of those people showed ways you could proceed, showed me different ways to go.

CR: Was Ted Hughes' work important to you? I'm thinking in particular of his early volumes.

KS: The early work was, yes. I guess they're nature poems, but certainly in those first books I thought the poetry was very exciting. The visual force of the description, the transformations – I'm thinking of 'The Thought Fox' – the reaction between him and the natural world, seemed to me to be very powerful. I liked his chances with language, with a sinuous use of language that took risks and seemed to make wide comparisons and that became with *Wodwo*, as an extension of *Lupercal* and *Hawk in the Rain*, confrontation with the implacable out there in nature and then in here with the self, with disaster. I admired his work and it was important to me.

CR: That said, did it irritate you at all to find yourself back in England in the middle 70s and corralled with others in Anthony Thwaite's round-up phrase 'the Tribe of Ted'?

KS: I was annoyed to be classified and pigeon-holed as a minor participant, but that was also a warning to get out of this "nature" slot. I felt that I had actually done so and that Thwaite was responding to very early poems, in particular one poem which I never even put in *The Poet Reclining* because I felt it didn't work properly.

CR: 'Both Harvests'.

KS: That was it. And so to be branded for all time by the British Council throughout the world, because that's what that publication meant, annoyed me, but it also alerted me to fight this tendency even more. I realised at the time that I had been writing a pastoral nostalgic lament for the country, whereas in fact I was a townsman. I remember realising this and deliberately forcing myself to look at the place I lived in, to look at the city around me, and to work from that rather than reflective old memory.

CR: With the publication of *Fox Running* in 1980 you moved very firmly into the city. The first editions of this poem have an accompanying note stating that it was part of a larger work in progress entitled *The Persistence of Vision*.

KS: *Fox* was *Fox* and never became part of a larger work. I'm always tending to project in this way and it doesn't happen. What it was is that this phrase, 'the persistence of vision', has so many possibilities of meaning. It is in the first place a technical term for the way images actually impact upon the eye making moving film possible. The man bouncing a ball in *Fox* is from the sequential photography of Eadweard Muybridge. He was one of the main pioneers of the experimental work showing how the retina can be tricked into seeing continuous motion where there is in fact a series of still pictures run at a precise speed. Technically that is called 'the persistence of vision'. But then the phrase itself appealed to me for evoking the idea of hanging onto a sense of the self, hanging onto a sense of one's own continuity. That is extremely important, certainly to Fox, and certainly to everyone, I think. So it came to have this secondary meaning as well. And then there's just vision itself. I believe in vision. Not just the optical experience, but seeing something suddenly burst into flame, burst into symbolic significance. That's what I call a vision. It's not angels ascending ladders but that you actually see something as it really is with all kinds of symbolic significance attached to it.

CR: This stressing of the need, the will, to search out continuity amidst fragmentation is surely encapsulated by those lines which I have always taken to be central not just to *Fox* but to all your work: 'Beginning again and again/ beginning from what's broken.'

KS: Beginning again is persisting. It is being persistent. Even though it fails you begin again because the alternative is to keep on going downwards. There's a lot of me in *Fox*. I was trying to get a grip of myself because I'd been on the run in London for quite a bit. It was only when I came to start writing it down that I began to get control over my own head and over my own life. So the writing was also accompanied by a growing sense of stability. I think what happens in *Fox Running* is that he is transformed, symbolically by faking his death – a metaphorical death of the former person. I'm still rather fond of the way he's now a kind of legend. He's 'glimpsed' – is he alive? is he dead? – but he's buried himself, and that whole business of the Underground is of course meant to evoke the under-world, is meant to have all the classic, mythical proportions to it.

CR: There's an allusion to *The Wanderer* in the closing lines of *Fox* – 'a wise man holds out'.

KS: I was absolutely conscious of ending the poem on that note because that then provides a continuity all the way back over a thousand years. It's still the same.

CR: Isn't there at the same time an affirmation of your trade, your craft: 'his enemies destroy themselves/ he defeats them with words'? This reinforces the earlier, 'I write or I die: that dramatic/ that simple.'

KS: I stand by those words very much: 'I write or die.' Dying in the sense of not necessarily physically dying but of suffering a mental or psychological death. I would be asleep in here. Nothing would be going on. To me, the whole thrill of being alive is growing old and learning. That to me is expressed through writing. Without it, I would cease to have an interaction with the world around me. Over the years I've come to rather like this very distant relation-ship secured through the work that goes out and gets read and sometimes comes back into my province again, sometimes years later. I rather like that. That to me is being part of the world and part of culture and society.

CR: Walls and borders, mental and physical, recur throughout your work. Is it fair to say that your obvious preoccupation with these and with how they impinge upon people's lives impacts upon your own mode of writing, breaking up the lyrical impetus, curbing the fullness of song? I'm thinking of 'Michi's song' and 'Dmitri's song' in *Wild Root*, but your use of this term goes back to *Work, distances* and the 'Death Songs/Death Dances'.

KS: They're metaphors, in a sense, dancing for moving, singing for speech or thought. For the North American Indians their dance was representative of their life, their song was their statement. A man made up a song for himself to sing at death. His song was the summation of his experience.

CR: You often seem to be glimpsing or coming upon the shards of a song.

KS: The decay of a song, the fragments of a song, the song that is highlighted in the memory because it is no longer possible to sing it, or you've forgotten the words, or the circumstances have changed. So 'Michi's song' and 'Dimitri's song' are similar in that, but there is a progressive contrast I think between them. Though, again, it's borders that do that, it's borders that fracture that song. Michi was from Voidovina, which was that province of Yugoslavia which was autonomous under old Yugoslavia until Milosovic annexed it. It's got a large Hungarian population, as it once was Hungarian, which is being pushed out. This is how they got rid of Michi, how they got him to move.

CR: The poem conveys this very starkly:

> Each night the phone rang.
> Sometimes silence, breathing. Or a man
> cursing in Serbian:
> why don't you go?
> You have a wife, children,
> we can kill them.
>
> You we will impale.

KS: Then they get his house; then they get his land. My interest in Hungary is stimulated by this business of borders and I focus in on that in the 'Wire Through the Heart' sequence in *Wild Root*. Hungary gets to be a Kingdom; Hungary gets to be an Empire. Yet Hungary is somehow not enough. It gets absorbed into Austria-Hungary but has borders around its population, and its minorities, whom the language excludes. The sense of identity is cemented through the language. Then, suddenly, once again Hungary is on the wrong side and they lose the war. They're now trapped within these much more confined borders with a lot of their co-Hungarians living outside. And how these different groups of Hungarians relate to the different governments they're under is what I find fascinating.

CR: The other major Hungarian poem in *Wild Root* is *The Shadow of God*, which alludes back specifically at one point to what we were talking about with reference to *Hawkwood*:

> Each with his patch to scratch, each
> his yard to guard, each with his own
> view of the world, his own particular opinion
> he will not give up easily.

KS: That's the dogs in Mohacs but, yes, I'm tying the two together, men and dogs. Wars begin with this.

CR: Masks in the poem are associated with the licensing of a form of wildness which is viewed as a necessary activity – I'm thinking of lines such as, 'wild in their tall wooden masks', 'the ruckus of men in the male dance', 'this is the management of chaos'.

KS: That's how we manage it. That's what I'm saying there. The idea of Saturnalia or the Lenten Carnival as a way of burning off the anger, the frustration, the excess, having a symbolic battle rather than a real war, dressing up and putting on masks so that you can be anonymous, ridiculous, drunk and stupid and make a lot of noise. You do that once a year maybe and that takes away the pressure. What the whole *Wild Root* book is about is exploring the idea of wildness: wildness as a necessary counterpart to civilisation. They are the complement of each other I think. Wildness existed before civilisation; civilisation is the denial of the Dionysian urge. You can't run around naked in the street, shouting and spitting and pissing and swearing, you can't have your own way. You can't be a Viking! As indeed one should not be, as indeed one should not be allowed to be. I do believe in civilisation. Yet, you put us in a city, you put us in a society, you put us in a nation, and there is still that wild urge. How is that to be dealt with? It's dealt with within this century by having enormously expensive and awful wars where people go crazy, but that's not it. The wildness is therefore modified by civilisation, but it's still the wildness. What I think goes through the book is that image of the wildmen in the Mohacs poem and of the procession of the homeless dead in the ghost poem, which re-occurs again and again and again as a theme, throughout Europe. In fact, throughout all civilisations there is this notion of those who are not included. Which, if you like, we can connect back to the idea of the outsiders, who have a perspective, who have a view-point, and we should listen to it.

CR: Stylistically, *The Shadow of God* is at times reminiscent of parts of *Fox Running* and 'At the solstice' from *Wormwood* in that there's that same sense of a driving vehement plainchant, of nominal and participle phrases being jammed together shorn of elaboration and connectives by a narrative urgency and commitment.

KS: There's a sort of English *ur* speech in my mind that is all of English, most of it spoken, much of it non-educated or language-conscious, and it's that speech, going all the way back to the Germanic, that I'm after at times, and hence there's an amalgam of Chaucer and Middle English, the Exeter Book and the Anglo-Saxon.

CR: I'm thinking of, for example, in *Fox*:

> Fox wanting to be alongwind
> amongst bracken his own shade...
> Being outlaw
> out classed out priced out manoeuvred
> hunger leashing him in to the city
> in the rattling milk bottle dawn

and in *The Shadow of God*:

> 300 cannon through the marches, some lost,
> the horses straining, the whips, no roads,
> no bridges in all this nowhere of mud,
> tracks that run to dead ends, watery graves...

CR: When you're writing this kind of material, are you conscious of drawing on something deep within?

KS: I'm on a roll. When I'm doing it, I know I'm on a roll. And I want to suspend any judgement, any criticism, any interference. That's when I'm most fluent and that's when I'm most enjoying myself. It's like playing an instrument, it's like playing jazz – another way of jamming, if you like. I think at those moments when I'm writing that kind of thing I am almost transparent. I am almost not here. OK, I'm sitting there operating that keyboard, but I'm just the instrument for this voice and I don't want to interpose at that point anything between me and what's coming up. I may do that later, but basically I just want the roll. I just want the sound of the language and of this voice coming through that isn't necessarily my voice, but comes through my voice. Sometimes I have a very strange sense of just being like a telephone exchange and these calls are coming through. I'm just trying to get them down on paper and capture the rhythm and the syntax and the exact words that I'm hearing.

DAVID CRYSTAL & TIM CUMMING
'Tough Shit Plato': The Ken Smith Interview

The interview with Ken took place in the late summer of 1986. He was just completing his 'first straight year' at Wormwood Scrubs as writer in residence, and was on the point of being sent down for another. *Terra*, his latest collection of poetry from Bloodaxe had come out, receiving good reviews in many papers and magazines.

It was in the wake of the Libyan bombings, of the Miners' Strike and its collapse, of the previous summer's riots, in the wake of these and Chernobyl, events which are important to Ken Smith and figure in his poetry and conversation, that this extensive interview was made.

The interview began with talk of the genesis of *Fox Running*, as Ken flicked through the original notebooks.

KS: All sorts of notes went towards the idea of a novel, and then it started as poem, and I dated it 15th January 1980, and called it 'Fox's Poems' and I dated it as I wrote it, from January to April.

Q: Did you write it in any kind of order?

KS: No, and that was a great discovery for me. I was taking a computer course at the time, and the whole non-linear idea of programming I found was like writing a novel. I realised 'I'm trying to write a poem and trying to start at the beginning and finish at the end' but the poems that come in my head and in my notebook don't come in that order. You've just got to get it down, and not think about where it's supposed to be. So at the end when I thought I'd got everything, it was a matter of typing up, numbering it, and spreading the entire thing out and gradually sorting the order it should go in. It was the first time I was able to do that. The serial order in which things are read is not that of which things are written.

Q: What scheme did you have for the order?

KS: There were nodes that particular parts or poems gathered around, and out of that there was a narrative developing. An inner narrative that I wasn't trying to express in the poem. I wasn't trying to tell the story of it. I was trying to arrange the "imagistic" events. The idea is a man (like me) coming up to London, can't get any work, can't get anywhere to live, the whole bloody shebang, but he's got this ghost-figure he keeps seeing, going the other way all the time. And this is his chance, because he finds him dead, and he looks like him, is him, so he swaps identities, swaps wallets. This is partly based on an incident in North London. There was a skinhead fight, and a bloke who was just a passenger on the train was knifed and killed and I chose him as the double in the poem.

The narrative story is the facts of this person's life, which could be anybody's, but when you meet a person you don't meet the facts of their life. You deal with that person as they come onto you.

Q: There's the exhaustion of the alcohol roam, all the bars.

KS: Yeah. That stems from working in a bar in Kilburn. I began to see people coming in who were in the position I had been in a couple of weeks before.

Q: Was Fox running away, only, or was there something to run to?

KS: Away. At this point in time there's nothing to run to. It's basically away from himself.

Q: I read Jeff Nuttall's remark about *Fox Running* being like jazz ('the poem is sustained by the kind of impulsive energy that sustains certain saxophone improvisations'). What do you think of that?

KS: I like that. The poem feels like music. In writing it I had a sense of it being like a tryptych with a fast section where he's going on the tubes and the trains, and surrounding slower ones.

(Talk about his prison work.)

Q: When people in prison start writing, it's like a paradox isn't it. They only start writing and delving into their imagination after they've been removed from the lives they've had. The awareness of life is perhaps much stronger because they're living in time, 'doing time', and not living in space.

KS: Yes it is, but the problem is how to relate it to anybody else. Blokes talk to me about the difficulty of writing letters. Say, there's one man who's trying to write to his father, and between him and the letter is the fact that he's in prison for murder, and how his father feels about that, and there's the thing where it must be like writing from one country to another. Never mind the language problem, say you're writing in English, there are so many things in the subtext that the person in the other country doesn't see or know that you would end up giving an endless explanation about 'the way we do things here'. And the guy says, 'I won't send you letters, there's nothing to write about. I can't say anything. I earned another four pence or something.' Has a shower.

They have this intensely private life in their head. I might see a bloke one Tuesday, and not see him again till next Thursday, and we've had a bit of a conversation, and he's referring to things I don't know about, which are in turn referring to the conversation we had before. He's got a mental record of it which is much better than mine and he's added to it, because in his head he's been talking to me and thinks he's actually said these things. It's a very strange insight into how my head works. I have conversations with people who aren't here all the time – and sometimes they turn into poems. But these men do it intensely and all the time. The more experienced cons get onto the less experienced ones and say 'watch out, you're doing it, you're walling yourself up', but I don't see any alternative to it.

There's a guy I know who's only been in since Easter, in his 50s, and when I first saw him he was totally out of it, had the traditional middle-class attitude to prisoners – he was a businessman – and he's now one of them. He was carrying himself around as he did outside, trying to get phonecalls, welfare, and so on, and he can't get any of it. So I spoke to him, gave him a cigarette, the first one he'd had, he hadn't got any baccy organised, and after seeing him over a period of time, you see him adjust to many years in jail. And there's nothing else you can do. Even though adjusting to it is giving in to it.

Q: In his case he was an outsider in an inside position.

KS: He has to adjust for his own survival, or he'll get punished by the screws, or by the other prisoners. But watching him make these adjustments and finding that I'm the jailor, I'm the guy saying 'you can't do that' disturbs me. It makes me wonder whether I should be doing the job. It may not be possible to write in prison. People have, but who are we talking about? Voltaire? Hitler? For me it comes back to the question of writing things down. Most writing that people want to read has to do with very dramatic moments and moments of great intensity – which are not the moments in which you write something down. In the middle of a fight you don't stop and take notes. And in those intensely dramatic situations, we are unselfconscious, we just act.

Q: But the mental image you retain afterwards may have the same, or similar, but transferred intensity.

KS: Yes, but that moment may extend quite some way down time. And with these guys it is like that.

Q: Do you see their writing as something for personal development, or do you actually see some good writers there? irrespective of their situation?

KS: I've seen one or two good writers there, but basically their situation prevents them from developing. For instance, I say to the prisoners, 'do what I do, I keep notebooks, write things down when they occur, when you overhear things'. But they can't do that. They don't have the privacy.

I remember something that Roy Fisher once said about working in a mental asylum – you just have to revise the parameters and reasons why you're doing this, and what writing is...you have to rethink it all. Is it to try and encourage talent, yes, is it to try and help people express themselves, yes – but suppose all they can express is very lame, mundane thought – but they've struggled like fuck to get this thought and write it down, well, it's like applauding the slower learner, you must reward that too. There's a degree of therapy in it, a degree of rehabilitation. I don't think you can separate these things out. There's a bit of both in all writing. But that is not the whole story. I don't write as a therapist. I write to find out who I am, to remember, to figure out where I've been, where I'm going. Apply that to the prisoner and you have good reasons for him doing it.

Q: There's a complete change between your first book *The Pity* and what you are doing now.

KS: I wrote *The Pity* between 1963 and 65. I don't think there was any particular political psychological event that occurred to change my writing. It was partly reconciling the fact that I'd moved to the city, and the feeling of embarrassment I had at being called 'a nature poet'. As the mirror does not lie, the reviewers who said that must have been telling the truth. But I'm not a nature poet. I'm *interested* in nature, but nature poetry means some kind of rural reserve, it's the whole ethos of pastoralism, which is something that occurs in the imagination when it is finished. When the population moves to the city they start writing sentimentally about the country, so the Sun King and Queen had their milkmaids and shepherds and fucked around in haystacks. I found the label terribly embarrassing. I thought 'yeah, it doesn't fit anywhere, because I live in cities, or there's something wrong with my work', and I really turned against *The Pity*.

Q: Returning to this first one after reading your other books, I thought 'my God, this is so out of context'.

KS: Yes, well that's where I began. Partly it was a delayed reaction. I grew up in the country, and when I moved to the city I was 13. And suddenly and dramatically there isn't this endless landscape to walk across, there's endless streets, but you can't see the horizon, it was brick and stone and unfriendly. And what I must have done was to have reverted to a dreamscape of childhood, and ten years go by and I'm still writing about it. It was a case of shaking my head very vigorously.

I think leaving England and going to the States was like a second displacement, getting as far away as I could. I tend to see culture as a series of paper bags. The immediate one is the family you grew up in and the circumstances. And then there's the neighbourhood, the houses, the district, which for me was the North of England. I couldn't understand the North of England until I went to the South of England, but then I couldn't begin to understand England until I got outside it. I didn't want to get outside to a non-English speaking place. I still wanted to be able to use the same language so I could compare the language as used there against the same language used here.

So you're moving outside these sets of parentheses, and though you can't see where you are, you can see where you were. So in my case I was someone who grew up, passed the eleven plus, escaped from the village, escaped from the working class – though I don't know if you can ever escape it, but you become divided from it – and I'm still running along this track that you get switched into when you're young and when you're about 27 years old you realise that you are on a track and what kind of track it is. Like going to do a degree, then teaching for four years and then realising this world is organised by people who think in linear ways.

That classical order of thought lies behind the *Pity* poems. Written by an average jerk who takes an English Literature degree and thinks in this serial, linear way and writes what Roger Garfitt calls 'the poetry of framed objects' which he designates as what is wrong with English poetry, it's framed objects, a meditation upon something, it's like looking at a photograph, whereas I am interested in a portrait that is not still, that is always moving. But I only discovered this when I was about 30. I think I was helped by teaching painters, who don't think in that framed or linear way. And that way of thinking is punished in schools. And I get the feeling we've all been sifted and filtered. So one lot go to work, the next get white collars, and so on. And I thought 'I don't want this, I don't want to be screened'. It didn't tell me what I wanted to do, but at least it told me what I wouldn't do.

Q: There's a poem in *Terra* that stands out, 'Roads in the north between two seas', which uses the memory of the landscape of your childhood, of the idealised *Pity* poems, but whose vision is much more mature.

KS: Well, it was consciously looking at it again.

Q: The long poem in *Terra*, *Hawkwood*, is set in a 14th-century situation, but I find it very contemporary in the "end of civilisation" environment Hawkwood is part of.

KS: It's the division of the heart from the brain. The genesis of the poem was that for a long time I'd been trying to find a way to write about these things. I don't think there's any point in trying to write about a nuclear holocaust. It's there every day in the back of the mind, and there's the strong possibility that it can end everything. To just write about it is a projection into the imaginary. The only thing you can do is read up on Hiroshima, and that's like camping in on someone else's experience. But I was reading a book mentioned in *Terra* in which there was a chapter on Hawkwood, and I identified with him. I began to hear his voice, which was the voice of an elderly regimental Sergeant-Major who has been through wars, seen lots of action, killed, nearly been killed, seen his mates killed, seen injustices, but he's still got some humanity about him. So I imagined what his journal might look like and I wrote the poems as his journal.

It was a bit like writing *Fox Running*. I find the way I work is that I have this imaginative structure, a plot, but I don't want to write a plot, a story, but it's a standpoint from which to write. So if I imagine this man's journal that he might write late at night in his tent – some entries might be after a battle, others before, others just in periods of lassitude, unemployment – but he writes it late at night, and he doesn't show anybody else. So I imagine I've found his journal. So I write what I imagine this journal to be, though I cheat and use contemporary references to make it relevant.

Q: In *Terra*, the *London Poems* describe a world of inverted values – I'm thinking of the poem that mentions 'the university of double glazing' the way people are obsessed with sale, with markets.

KS: What they are doing is preying on people's intimidation. So if you go to the university of double glazing, it's a double inversion. It has that double meaning of what is going on in universities anyway. And they are researching very frightening things – crowd control, people control.

(*Ken went on to discuss policing, the Miner's Strike, Notting Hill, and the incidents of helicopter raids made on Canning Town and Broadwater Farm, summer 1986.*)

…but it all has its logic and its rhetoric. They have new equipment and they have to test it, so they need a situation to test it in. There was a manufactured riot in Brixton. It was done to test the system they had just set up. The media select the incident. 'There is a riot going on in Brixton, the police have the upper hand.' They don't say *why* there's a riot, because they've decided to demolish three houses that people were living in – no matter what they were alleged to be doing – allegations that have no proof, in the same way that when we bombed Libya we had no proof of the reason. And the news is often no news at all. The story that stuck in my mind from a few weeks ago was the Queen Mother has been taken to hospital in a helicopter because she's got something stuck in her throat. It struck me as amazing. I timed it, and it went on for 6 minutes. Who is this old woman who eats too much, who drinks gin and tonic, until it pours out of her ears – why should she be carried 130 miles in a helicopter?

The book I'm trying to write is a prose journal of the year I've done in the Scrubs – I've just finished 52 straight weeks – and that's what I'm calling the journal. And what I'm trying to do is to write the outside as the inside. They are incompatible in an odd sort of writing way. When I get a day to myself and try to write about the Scrubs, it's so remote, the whole lot just recedes. It's this dream in the distance, receding as the world recedes once you're inside. The inmates say 'the outside, that's unreality, we don't think about it'. Because if you do think about it, it'll only be distorted.

Another bloke said that whatever you do you've always got a wall down the middle of your face. It's a split vision. Which is an idea I use in *Fox Running*. It's the division of the retina and also a psychic division, between the world you have to live in and the world you're living in up in your head. Which is where I'm living most of the time. You're just a creature that's conscious of itself and its existence. And possibly the only ones in the whole of space and time. You can travel, know other people, and that's fraught with a great deal of difficulty and problems always. And the idea is that you just want to be free.

Q: There's a self-awareness on one side, and on the other, total obscurity.

KS: That's what I mean by the split vision. I privately wonder whether we are aberrant. I'm thinking particularly of the white, Anglo-Saxon, Northern European kind of man who because of climate and conditions had to go elsewhere and kick others in the head and steal their dinner. The Vikings, the Luthers, the Calvins. But these are now the norms of the world. Extended by the North Americans. The old split between the "angst" of the north and the calm of the south – for the seasons are in their favour – is gone now. There's an essay by Lawrence comparing the barrack squares he grew up in with the piazzas, walkways, covered areas of an Italian city. Now I wonder if the whole world is aberrant.

But consider Jung. Jung is a gift, really, he considers the things that the modern man of technological advancement doesn't. 'Synchronicity' is a very late Jung essay. He wrote that what we see is only the surface, and the deeper meaning, the deeper substance of what is going on can sometimes be recognised through signs, multiple feelings, symbols, feelings you have about places, people, things, and that one has to trust these feelings as much as one trusts analytical thought. One of the ways is to recognise coincidence, which is what synchronicity is. I tend to take notice when something happens three times. Or when something very similar happens. We usually say 'oh it's just coincidence'. But Jung is suggesting that there is a different structure to the world that we can't see.

For after all, who are we? We're animals who happen to perceive in certain ways, orally, visually, and by smell and touch, but we are basically creatures that are adapted for hunting in packs, though technologically we are much further on than that. Hundreds of years being peasants, and 150 years of being citified which is a very short amount of time, and we haven't cancelled out what we are, which is why I think people go on football riots. It's kind of necessary. You can see that it's just another version of what happened in Hawkwood's time. All the blokes would get together and raid France. And you might come back rich and be made for life. Chaucer was one such man who went on a raid into France, so I used a couplet by him at the beginning of Hawkwood, because this is what he said when he came back:

> There is ful many a man that crieth Werre Werre
> That would ful litel what were amounteth.

Q: That idea of violence – I remember working with a bloke who said to me 'what would you if you had AIDS?' And I said 'I'm not sure' and he says, 'I know what I would do, I'd go and rape and do all the looting I could before I died.'

KS: God!...(*Incredulous laughter.*) It's frightening isn't it – but you see, that is it, it's there. There's no difference in time. Nothing has changed. All we see is an illusion, all this technology, all this city, it's here, it generates its own conditions but there's that basic underneath aggression. It adapts itself to any environment. That's what I find dealing with these blokes in the nick and the reasons they got here. Liberals say 'it shouldn't be' but that is the most useless statement, you might as well fart. 'Should' and 'ought to', *should* be got rid of…we should not say should. You cannot get rid of the problem by ignoring it. Most of life is noise, aggression and establishing your territory. The way animals and birds behave.

Q: Is there a solution, a way to channel the aggression to positive ends, to make it less destructive?

KS: I don't know. That's a good question and I don't know the answer. Supposing there isn't?

The playwright I like most is David Rudkin. There's a play I do remember very vividly called *Afore Night Come*, and it's based upon the last known witchcraft killing in 1923-24, in Devon, a hedger was found with a three-pronged fork in his neck. But in this play, it's an apple-picking, apple harvest, with hired labour, day labour, unemployed whatever, and it's just their dialogue and it builds and builds and eventually there is a sacrifice, eventually there is a young man hanging on a tree. Sacrifice. Christianity, and all the religions, have some symbol of sacrifice. And you can't ignore the archetypes.

But in the analytical consciousness it is dead. The archetype, the myth has come now to mean its opposite. And that's the arrogance and terrible ignorance of the present. If it's mythic, you'd better pay attention to it, because it's something that occurs in different cultures, it must mean something, god knows what, but to acknowledge it is much better than denying it.

Q: There's the George Eliot phrase 'the web of life' – the cultural systems, not just moral or personal things. *Hawkwood* has that kind of split we have been talking about. In the poem there is the image of his heart, his private vision.

KS: Mmm. I was thinking of him being in Italy, thinking of her, his heart, flying over the Alps to England – the 'snowy passes she will die in' or 'like me, sell her only skin' – she'll have to whore, as he does. He's a male whore as a soldier, a mercenary. But my theory about the 'split', the aberration is that we are way out of line with the planet we live on, the society we're in, the lie we have, we're on a dead road and we're going to blow it all up.

(*Ken proceeded to talk about nuclear fear. News reports [the interview took place during the Libyan crisis]. Delayed Falklands reportage.*)

KS: Now they manipulate warfare so that they can order. It's like in the Miners' Strike, the police provoked a situation, and the film crews recorded the result, they didn't record the cause. Gadafy did the same thing during the Embassy siege here in London. It's the same manipulation of images. One of the things that has intrigued me about working in the prison and talking to them about their cases is the fact that objects are sometimes shown to a jury which is not the object in question, say a knife that is not the murder weapon, because the knife is only four inches long and the wound is five inches deep. But it is found on the premises, it has no fingerprints, there's no blood on it, it's totally irrelevant. But it sways the jury. The gun, the knife, it is an image, even if the gun or knife never killed anybody. It's a focusing. 'Focus on this' in the same way that we're politically manipulated. 'Think about Libya, think about a bombed nightclub, think about a sergeant that's killed.' And right, let's bomb Libya. We might all die for this. But think in these ways. Think about now, never about the past.

When you think about former attitudes to the past, they become very interesting. Here's one story for instance. In Ripon Minster they have some beautiful woodcarvings, reliefs. Most of them are Biblical scenes, the Red Sea parting and so on, but there was one that was looking down on a man with a wheelbarrow with another person in it. Surrounded by leaves, and birds, and so on, but I couldn't work out what it meant. Apparently (and the Church had only just discovered this) it was this Saxon saint in the 8th Century A.D. He was a shepherd on Exmoor. His father dies, his mother is sick, and he finds he can't both tend his sheep and look after his mother, so he decides in perfectly logical fashion, to put his mother in a wheelbarrow and wheel it all the way across southern England to some place in Sussex where the wheelbarrow fell to bits. And where it falls to bits, he builds a chapel, preaches to the heathen and converts them. And I thought 'this is a story about a lunatic wheeling a barrow across the country with his sick mother in it' and this story, that stems from the 8th century is recorded in the north of England in the 15th century. And it's a totally different timescale – about 700 years (the distance from Homer to Troy, as a matter of fact.) We don't have that any more. If we think back 700 years it's 1206. I can't think about those people. We can barely go back to the last century, can barely go back before birth. Somehow the current ethic is to simply live in the present. Which somehow robs the consequences of their actions.

Q: History is taught as a linear movement of dates. The people and the story of people's lives is removed.

KS: One is accustomed, when growing up, of thinking people, anybody, in history, who happened to be dead as different somehow. But toothache felt like toothache, sexual craziness like sexual craziness.

The song of the blackbird must have had the same impact.

Q: As with myths, so with history, it becomes a story and not a truth.

KS: It's as if we've somehow managed to focus on the present which we know is ephemeral, and have managed to exclude everything else. We can be extremely analytical about all sorts of things within narrow areas, and totally ignore so much else which is fatal.

One of the seminal experiences I had, which has to do with loss of the language in which you communicate, is a week I spent in Spain, in Pamplona, the city they run the bulls in, chasing a job that actually came to nothing and I spent one day in Bilbão, which is very strange because it's Basque country. And Basques are totally different from Europeans. There were differences that you weren't looking for, in the use of colour, their eyes move differently, their facial gestures. I went from bar to bar, getting drunk on my last pesetas, and I was getting into conversations that were not direct because there was no language in common – Basques don't speak Spanish. They taught me so much. For one thing, something about nuclear power. It is the power of the sun. It's Prometheus stealing from the gods. It's nothing to do with us. There is no container for it. They are sun-worshipping people, basically. Their symbol is a sun sign, which in fact is an inverted swastika. It's a wind sign, a flowing sign. But we are not perfect, and the power of the sun, nuclear power, has to be handled perfectly. Yet here we are with the arrogance to be burdened with this technology which is going to destroy. We can't control it.

I find more and more that just the act of writing, the choice to use language becomes the choice of which "myth" (in the derogatory sense) you use, the one about science solving all our problems, the political one about socialism, sorry, that's a sad dream too, that's bureaucracy, people who are not connected with the products of their labour. I think the act of having hope is a piece of political cheekaboo (sic). But supposing there isn't hope? Suppose we're the last generation on earth, perhaps all there ever might be in the universe, in terms of consciousness. Tough shit Plato...goodbye to all that – that is what I meant in *Fox Running*...goodbye search for the unified feeling, all those things, all that effort.

Q: The problem is all the obstacles to even a small change.

KS: I don't see that you can do it any more. I don't think there is any chance of change.

POEMS FOR KEN

Ken in the back garden at Friars Road with Tony Connor, 2001

Raven Beck

ken I ran across fells to Raven Beck
heather, tufts of reeds, shake holes, rocks –
and jumped fences to get you a feather
to bring you back from the driving sleep
where black birds fly in black air
and black waters fall in black ravines
I brought you a feather Ken
so you can speak with the short-eared owls
so you can bind root in rock with hawthorn
so you can skim the wind with peregrine
so you can box with the hare
and dance with the fox

TOM PICKARD
22 February 2003

Railway Hotel
(for Ken)

Why this hotel, and this town and this province of X
On this night in the Year of the Turnip? Why
This name and this face in the passport? Well?

Out there the foggy road still curves away
Across the railway tracks. Young birches in the sidings.
Sounds of shunting, off in the rusty damp.

The suitcase. Full of books? It could as easily
Be drill-bits, lenses, chocolate.
You must be travelling in something. *Time,*

You say, flicking the locks to inspect
The interior. Something that glows? You give
Nothing away. It goes under the bed again.

Down at the end of the hall is a wolf in a case,
Howling at the moon in 1910, illuminated
By the beer sign in the street. Perhaps

It went like this: you stopped for dinner here
To view the curiosities, and this
Was one of them. You never know.

At her high desk the red-haired proprietress
Sits in a draught with the radio doing a polka
To death, and once again she's gotten

Lipstick on her teeth. And nothing happens
For a hundred years but fog and shunting,
Lipstick and polkas, the half-lives

Of objects marooned by imagined
Utility. *So, are we going, or what?*

SEAN O'BRIEN
28 March 2003

Objects in a Row:

Ken Smith, Reading

three stones, one blue feather,
a piece of polished driftwood,
thin and white as bone, two

shells, convex and dark at their
centers, like eyes lifted out of
the sea; each thing accounted for,

named, then set down along
the front edge of the table, stone,
driftwood, feather and seashell

horizon; his palms opened out,
everything, that is, shown,
given up to table, sightline, speech;

pages lifted into the long reach
of breath in flight: *birds, trees,
men & women*, what small sound

cupped and lifted to the ear's driftwood
plate, *the world declaring itself
landscape moment distance whole*

MICHAEL ANANIA
12 May 2003

Meeting and Missing

(in memoriam K.S.)

It might have been you I saw
in the *Apostelok Hotel*
in *Attila József Utca*,
sitting among the local whores
and Arab arms dealers:
a man with the look of absence on his face,
seeking his own curled self in another place.

And what about that time
we arranged a secret meeting
at *Eine Kleine Kartoffel*
in Bad Godesberg, or somewhere
else bad in Germany?
I was of Baker Abel Oboe Roger,
you in the youthful blue of an up-stager.

If, indeed, that was you
and not some slippery you S. of A.,
as later among the guy talk,
the high, boozy, rockin' talk,
driven for out-of-county –
a blur of big ambition and petty need
to be written, published, hated, put to bed.

Back with your old mates,
back where, perhaps, you belonged,
did I meet you in a pub –
Jack Smartarse and Joe Dickhead
glued to the TV,
while you and a smoky man with a face like mine
talked of death and the use of the semi-colon?

Then, if one of us wasted years
in the Enterprise Zone,
the other pumped iron
in the annexe of unease
until he completely forgot
what he was training for. That's how we poets –
oracular, banal, – finish up old sots.

Delete *old sots.*
Go straight to prison. Press *Enter,*
retain the crumpled scratchcard
as evidence for the Inland Revenue.
Now print our pensioners' skill
amid a darkening garden's many greens:
construers of loss and gut-aches, love and knee-pains.

And now a different darkening
under hospital bright lights,
the words fast running out –
just a few good jokes left,
some over-the-glasses looks
and the lost, last chance at games we never played
in Leeds long ago and wherever it was Leeds led.

Cancel word-play. Substitute
Vijay Bharati, Homer Simpson,
the nurse with a big bottom.
Ignore all rhymes and metrical structures.
Delete previous emails,
frontiers, gypsies, Friars Road, the sweet
fragrance of shed-side blossom, friends. Delete.

TONY CONNOR
28 July 2003

Ghost Notes

Don't look for me. I've gone to ground, the fox to its hole.
KEN SMITH

1

So this is it, the it
we always talked about,
the invisible moment of transition
from here – warm and breathing, words
on your tongue of thought –
to gone from here, forever cold, silent.
The seamlessness as we watched you
run out of air, all our hopes evaporating.
Out of our control. Never was up to us, alone.

2

Now there's only one story to tell,
the one where you popped your clogs,
cashed in your chips, snuffed it,
bought the ranch, kicked the bucket,
went to the Happy Hunting Grounds,
fell asleep, passed over, shuffled off
down the long pale corridor, through the Pearly Gates,
met your Maker, met the boatman,
crossed the river Styx, and stones,
you break my heart. Brown bread. Dead you know.

3

What's it like where you are
in the suspected nothingness of non-think,
no dreams, no insomnia, no frettings
for the state of the world, going to hell
in its own hand cart of corpulence, opulence,
greed, rubbing the bones on the other
side of the street, deprivation, starvation,
desperation. No need of sleep, or drink or eat,
no nicotine cravings, no voda, no vodka, alas.
No anger, no crossed arms saying *I'm going home*,
some imagined quarrel, your mother's set of the jaw,
some character in your head.

163

All the news, one troubled lie
you can't untangle, nor I.
No more fear of failure, of finances,
of not being loved or seen or heard.
No more fear of growing old, mindless, legless –
no more fearing death, how it will come.
No, you pass that baton down to me.

4

The dead speak through me, you said.
So speak to me now. Tell me about your journey,
the third wall, the one you couldn't tear down,
break through, go around or over or under.
Not even you, with your indomitable spirit,
could win the final war.
None of the battle books you read,
prepared you for this one – not Mohachs,
not Culloden, not Sarajevo,
Afghanistan, Iraq, the promise
of all those to come. No.

5

Death's your final journey my love.
Single ticket. No reports back
from you of the endless conversation.
Shut up, it's a story,
your fist on the counter, laughing,
amazed after all these years
that we had so much to say to each other,
such urgency, such passion. Words tumbled us to sleep.
It doesn't stop. Love didn't die with you.
No. But where's the music from this strange place,
where's the speech, the rhythm of the language,
the jokes. Or is it soundless too.

6

Out here in this so real realm called life,
it's surreal that this mound of your remains
brings such comfort. There's nothing more
I can do for you, but go on being for you.
Let's just have a little peace and light, you said.

And here it is, this copse of trees, shading,
waving in a breeze, sound of a windchime, birdsong.
Just such a spot you and I'd have sat,
scribbling in our notebooks, day-walking,
sleep-dreaming, thief-listening
to the long grass, a fox, running still.
A grape, a chunk of cheese I place,
lay a flower on your chest.

7

Love doesn't conquer all.
But the loss of love
conquers us all.
And I have to concede
that not all my love could keep you alive.
Death, no stranger to our conversation,
ran with its bushy tail through your poetry.

8

Some of the grandsons say you came back as butterfly,
blessing their shoulders one by one,
Arnez, Arnoux, Aran. Blue spot on brown.

Some hear you speak between wave break,
foam crash, see you as cloud gathering
an audience. They listen.

Your daughter takes you whole and healed
into her meditation hut,
blesses you with water.

Your son hears anew what you always said to him,
feels the resonance of your spirit.
His heart begins to move his feet.

Perhaps it was some spirit of yours
in guise of fox, running the length
of the funeral procession. Foxes abounded

passing your spirit into our acceptance.
Though we can't, and why should we,
ever stop missing you.

9

I dream you alive, us dancing, the feel of your firm,
the fine of your bones, your smell,
the timbre of your voice in my ear,

my heart in my throat, as I wake to the end
of it all, again. Every out is just in again
to the presence of your absence.

Every place I go, just another without you.
But for that beat in my heart
which doesn't want to.

A peacefulness guides me imperceptibly.
Sorrow is the tears in the heart
that never make it to the eyes.

10

Gone now, back to the rain, the good earth,
the wild tangle of plants, ivy, holly,
growing in the absence of your presence.

The darkness stumbles into me.
The darkness stumbles us all
into a make-believe light.

And who in the end,
do I tell it all to,
if not you.

JUDI BENSON

Ken at the memorial event for Izet Sarajlic, Sarajevo, October 2002.